The Cow of No Color

THE COW

OF NO COLOR

Riddle Stories
and Justice Tales from
Around the World

Nina Jaffe and Steve Zeitlin

Pictures by Whitney Sherman

Henry Holt and Company

New York

Henry Holt and Company, Inc., *Publishers since 1866*
115 West 18th Street, New York, New York 10011

Henry Holt is a registered trademark of Henry Holt and Company, Inc.
Text copyright © 1998 by Nina Jaffe and Steve Zeitlin
Illustrations copyright © 1998 by Whitney Sherman
All rights reserved.
Published in Canada by Fitzhenry & Whiteside Ltd.,
195 Allstate Parkway, Markham, Ontario L3R 4T8.

Library of Congress Cataloging-in-Publication Data
Jaffe, Nina.
The cow of no color: riddle stories and justice tales
from around the world / by Nina Jaffe and Steve Zeitlin.
p.   cm.
Includes bibliographical references.
Summary: In each of these stories, collected from around
the world, a character faces a problem situation which
requires that he make a decision about what is fair or just.
1. Children's stories. [1. Fairness—Fiction. 2. Justice—
Fiction. 3. Short stories.] I. Zeitlin, Steven J. II. Title.
PZ5.J256Co 1998 [Fic]—dc21 98-14167

ISBN 0-8050-3736-5 / First Edition—1998
Designed by Martha Rago
Printed in the United States of America on acid-free paper.∞
1 2 3 4 5 6 7 8 9 10

The authors are grateful to the many people—friends, colleagues, story-tellers, and scholars—who helped make this collection possible. Some of these people are noted in story introductions and source notes, but we would especially like to thank Rabbi Edward Schecter, Judith Gleason, Mai Vo-Dinh, and Yami Vang for story sources and references.

We are indebted to Li Chi Ho, Lisa Lindsay, Rachel Kramer, Dorian Segure, and Mark Stein—teachers and graduate students at Bank Street College of Education—for invaluable assistance in research and revisions; to Amanda Dargan and the staff of City Lore for being on call; to folklorist Ilana Harlow and her father, Rabbi Jules Harlow, for passing on midrashic commentary about justice and mercy; to Sam Schrager for sharing his research on storytelling by trial lawyers; and especially to Jonathan Moore, whose work as a defense lawyer and interest in the power of folktales was a key inspiration for this book.

Many thanks are due to our editor, Marc Aronson, for contributing a story, for his gentle but persistent nudging, and for his insights; to our agent, Carla Glasser; and especially to our children—Ben and Eliza Zeitlin, and Louis Jaffe Armistead—who always ask the right questions.

* * * *

For Tom Roderick, Maxine Phillips, and their two wonderful daughters, Emma Rose and Anne Marie, with love.
—N. J.

For my brothers, Murray and Bill.
—S. Z.

෧෧෧෧෧෧෧෧ Contents

Introduction   3

Poetic Justice: A Taste of Their Own Medicine   9
   The Cow of No Color/Ghana   10
   The Sound of Work/The Balkans   14
   Ximen Bao and the River Spirit/China   18
   The Cloak/Ireland   23

Bringing Wrongdoers to Justice:
Matters of Guilt and Innocence   27
   The Thief and the Pig/China   28
   The Testimony of the Fly/Vietnam   32
   Susannah and the Elders/Ancient Israel   40
   The Jury/United States   47

Forgiveness and Mercy: Throwing the First Stone   53
   The Magic Seed/The Middle East   55
   The Bird Lovers/Laos   59
   An Ounce of Mud/Eastern Europe   70

Settling Disputes: Between a Rock
and a Hard Place   75
   The Dance of Elegba/Nigeria, Cuba   76
   The Three Wives of Nenpetro/
   Central Africa   84
   The Flask/Ancient Israel,
   Eastern Europe   88

Deciding Ownership: Who Owns the Sky?   93
　Kim Son Dal and the Water-Carriers/
　Korea   94
　The Land/Ancient Israel,
　Eastern Europe   99

Cosmic Justice: The Big Questions   103
　Sharing the Soup/Mexico   104
　A Higher Truth/Syria   110
　The Walnut and the Pumpkin/India   114

You're It!: The Playground and Beyond   117
　The Wise King/United States   118
　Josephus in the Cave/Ancient Israel   122
　The Water Pot and the Necklace/
　Nigeria   128
　The Test/United States   134

Epilogue   137

Source Notes   139

Bibliography   153

Resources and Organizations   161

The Cow of No Color

Introduction

According to the ancient Egyptian *Book of the Dead*, when a pharaoh died, he was placed on a boat mounted on wheels that was pulled by oxen into his tomb. After the tomb was sealed, the dead man's soul traveled to the underworld, where an assemblage of gods and goddesses sat in judgment at the throne of the goddess Maat. The goddess held an ankh and scepter, and wore a beautiful ostrich feather on her head. Before each soul lay the fabled scales of justice. Today, a scale is a thin plastic box that you step on to weigh yourself. But for most of human history, scales were a set of balances where an object was placed on one side to be weighed, and balanced against a set of known weights on the other.

The god Anubis, Lord of Mummy Wrapping, with the body of a human and the head of a jackal, stood beside the goddess. His appointed task was to weigh each human heart on the scales of justice. At the right of the balance, behind Anubis, stood Thoth, the scribe of the gods, holding his reed pen and papyrus to record the result of the trial. Upon the beam of the scales sat a dog-headed ape.

At the trial of souls, the dead person's heart was placed on one side of the scales, the ostrich feather from Maat's headdress on the other. The feather represented justice and truth. The heart represented the dead soul's conscience. An ideal heart was neither too heavy nor too light to balance against the feather. The dog-headed ape watched the pointer and told Thoth when the beam was exactly level. If the scale tipped to the left or the right, the heart failed the test, and was immediately devoured by Ammit, "eater of the dead," a ferocious animal with the head of a crocodile, the body of a lion, and the rump of a hippo. If the soul held in perfect balance with the feather of justice and truth, the god Thoth took note, and the dead soul approached immortality.

From ancient times down through the present, scales have been a symbol of justice. Our system of justice weighs the evidence and determines a person's guilt or innocence. In courtrooms, justice is often portrayed as a blindfolded woman holding a set of scales. In some religious traditions, people believe that a person's good deeds will be balanced against his or her bad deeds on a day of judgment.

Every day, whether we are adults or children, we have to make difficult choices to decide what is wrong and what is right. Should I share this cupcake with my friend or keep it for myself? Should I give up my seat to a senior citizen who has just walked onto the crowded bus? If I see someone being cruel to an animal, should I tell him to stop or should I just walk away? If someone pushes herself ahead of me on line at school, do I jump in front of her? Should I call the teacher? Or should I just let it go? Every day, human beings are confronted with these decisions. Sometimes they are small, and affect only you and your friends and family. Sometimes these choices can affect all the people in your community, and even the whole country.

All over the world, as long as human beings have lived together in groups, they have had to ponder questions of fairness. Different cultures and groups of people have different systems of law and ways of working out solutions to complicated situations. Sometimes what might seem a strange or unfair law to you might be considered correct and proper in another country.

Decisions about what is just are never easy. The famous American lawyer Clarence Darrow once said, "Is there anybody who knows what justice is? No one on earth can measure out justice. Can you look at any man and say what he deserves—whether he deserves hanging by the neck until dead, or life in prison, or thirty days in prison, or a medal?"

In this book, we have gathered stories from different corners of the globe. In each story, the characters are faced with a problem or a situation that revolves around figuring out what is fair or unfair. Sometimes the tales are riddle stories that ask the listeners to think about a problem in new and unusual ways. Some of these stories have been used by lawyers defending their clients in courts of law; some of them are based on real historical characters; and others take place in legendary kingdoms. But in all of them we ask you: "What would you do if you were in this story? How would you solve the characters' dilemma so that justice wins out in the end?"

To read this book, you will need an imaginary set

of those fabled scales of justice as you try to decide whether a poor man of the Middle East should hang for stealing a piece of bread, whether to answer a knock on the door in an old Mexican folktale, and how to bring a West African chief a "cow of no color."

⇥⇥⊙⇥⇥⊙⇥⇥⊙ Poetic Justice: A Taste of Their Own Medicine

Justice comes in many colors. One ancient principle of justice was first set forth in the Old Testament of the Bible: "An eye for an eye, a tooth for a tooth." The stories in this section, including our title story, "The Cow of No Color," provide another kind of justice, what is sometimes called "poetic justice." In these stories, the villains get their just deserts in a symbolic and imaginative way. The punishment is the perfect answer to the crime: it not only "punishes" the villains but teaches them a lesson.

The Cow of No Color

(G h a n a)

In Africa, storytelling has long been important, not only for entertainment but also as a way of passing on history, values, and family traditions. In Nigeria, people who had to settle a case before the chief often used proverbs to explain their evidence or defend their point of view. The wise and clever use of proverbs could often determine the outcome of cases brought before the chief and elders. In Ghana, riddles and proverbs are used to help children learn how to think creatively. This story was told to Nina by Gideon Foli Alorwoyie, a master drummer, who learned it from his grandmother when he was a boy.

Once among the Ewe people of Ghana there lived a wise woman named Nunyala. For miles around, people would come to her asking for advice, and she always found a way to help them. Her fame spread till it reached the ears of the chief, who became very jealous. He called her to the palace, and when she appeared, he said to her, through his spokesman:

"I hear you are Nunyala, the wise woman."

"That may be, and that may not be," she replied. "It is what some people say."

"If you are so wise," said the chief, "surely I can ask you to do one simple thing for me."

"If it is simple or not," she replied, "I will do my best."

"All you have to do to prove how wise you are," the chief said to her, "is to bring me a cow."

Nunyala thought to herself: "A cow. That is not difficult. My village is full of cows."

And she was just about to leave when the chief added, "Now listen well. Yes, I wish you to bring me a cow. But this cow cannot be black, and it cannot be white. It cannot be brown, or yellow, or spotted, or striped. In fact, this cow cannot be of any color at all! Bring me a cow of no color in three days' time—or you will be executed without delay!"

―――――――――――――――――――――――――――――――

Nunyala returned to her village and sat in her hut. She thought to herself: Should I be executed be-

cause some people say I am as wise as the chief? Should I lose my own life for his jealousy? Is this a wise leader's approach to justice? She had to answer the chief's impossible request, but how?

Nunyala sat and thought for three days and three nights, and at the end of that time, she sent a child from her village to the chief with a message. The chief sat on his stool, waiting to hear what the child had to say. These were his words: "O Chief, Nunyala, the wise woman of our village, has sent me to repeat these words to you. This is her message. She has said, 'I have your cow of no color. It is in my house. You can come and take it.

"'But don't come in the morning. Don't come in the evening. Don't come at dawn. Don't come at twilight. Don't come at midnight. Don't come any time. You can have your cow of no color—at no time at all!'"

The boy turned and left the palace, while the chief sat speechless on his stool, to ponder the words of Nunyala, wise woman of the Ewe.

The Sound of Work

(The Balkans)

Joha is a famous fool who lives in Turkish and Arabic folktales. In 1492, the Jews of Spain (called Sephardic Jews) were expelled from that country for their religious beliefs. Many of them settled in the Ottoman Empire, part of which is now Turkey. These Jewish communities adapted Joha for their own stories.

Joseph Elias's family was among those who fled from Spain and settled in the town of Monastir in the Ottoman Empire. The town was later part of Yugoslavia, now Macedonia. Prior to World War I, Joseph's father came to America. Joe Elias, now a renowned singer of Sephardic music, was born on the Lower East Side of New York City in 1933. This is where he heard the Joha stories from his father: "My father wouldn't formally tell Joha stories. It's not like he sat us down and said, 'Now I am going to tell a story.' It's like when somebody breaks an egg, for example—that's a time to tell a broken-egg story. With seven kids in the house, opportunities to drop an egg are many."

This is a tale of Joha that Joseph Elias's father told him in Ladino, the Spanish-derived language of Sephardic Jews. Joe passed it on to us so that we could tell it to you.

━━━━━━━━━━━━━━━━━━━━━━━━━━━━━━━━━

So you want some tales of Joha? Joha was looking for work, and there was a man who had a job for someone to split wood with an ax. A heavy-duty job. But Joha really didn't have his heart set on doing such heavy manual labor. Just then, a *casalino* (a peasant) comes along who wants the job. The problem is that the *casalino* is mute. So the foreman motions to him what they need him to do.

That gives Joha an idea. He tells the boss, "The two of us will make a pair. Because he's mute, I will help him out." So the *casalino* takes the ax and he begins to chop. And with every blow, Joha goes, "Uhh!" He grunts. The mute man swings the ax and Joha grunts, "Uhh!" And he swings the ax and he grunts, "Uhh!" So all day long the *casalino* is chopping wood and Joha is grunting, "Uhh!"

At the end of the day, the boss arrives with the pay for splitting wood. He gives the money to the *casalino*. Joha says, "Wait a second, this is a two-man job. I should get paid half the salary! He does the swinging and I do the 'Uhh!'" The boss man is not at all sure about this line of reasoning.

So the boss takes them to a judge, and the judge says, "Tell me what happened." So the mute man stands there, and Joha says, *"Este aqui no puede ablar*—this man doesn't speak. He was swinging the ax, and I was going, 'Uhh!' With every blow, every blow, he swung and I went, 'Uhh!' I should get paid my share."

The judge smiled. Then he meted out the perfect reward.

━━━━━━━━━━━━━━━━━━━━━━━━━━━━━━

Can you guess how the judge rewarded Joha for his labor?

The judge says, "Bring me the sack of money. Bring it over here now, in front of me." And the judge pours the coins slowly from the sack into a brass bowl. Piece by piece they clink against the sides. Joha reaches for the money. The judge says, "No, no, no, you don't touch the money. You already got paid."

Joha says, "What do you mean?"

The judge says, "For the sound of work, you hear the sound of money. But money you don't get."

. . . .

Joha, who tries to outsmart everyone else, gets outsmarted himself in many of these stories.

Ximen Bao and the River Spirit

(China)

*Throughout the history of ancient China, the em-
perors would send special officials to all parts of
the land to carry out the laws and keep order in
the towns and the surrounding areas. These magistrates had great powers. They acted as judges
and tax collectors and oversaw many details in
the lives of the people under their jurisdiction.
Some of them were cruel and abused their powers.
Ximen Bao was known as a wise and just man
who used his office to help the people. This story,
told to Nina by Li Chi Ho, a teacher and native
of Taiwan, is one of the most well-known stories
about Ximen Bao. Li Chi Ho first heard it when
she was a child.*

O ne year, Ximen Bao was sent as a magistrate to
Ye County in northern China. In one of the
towns he went to visit he saw that the people were
very sad. Their crops were meager and the market-

place empty of customers. He asked the town officials why the people looked so unhappy. One of the officials spoke and said: "We have suffered greatly in this town for many years because we are forced to marry young girls to the river spirit. The three elders of this town tax us on all our possessions. They have collected many thousands of coins from us. They use some of this money for marrying young girls to the river spirit. The rest they keep for themselves. There is a priestess in the village, who serves as medium between the people and the deities. The officials pay her to choose the young girls. If the priestess sees a pretty girl, even in the house of a peasant, she will take her from her family. She will give her silk clothes, food and drink, and keep her in a pavilion near the river. Then the priestess and her followers will bind the young girl to a bed and push it off from shore. After the bed drifts for a while, it sinks down to the bottom of the river. Many of our families with young daughters have fled. This is why our streets are so empty, our houses so poor, and our lives so sad."

Ximen Bao nodded. Then he asked, "What if you refuse?" The officials shook their heads. "No, we cannot, for there is a saying: 'If we do not marry girls to the river spirit, there will be a flood and all the people will drown.'"

Ximen Bao said, "The next time the villagers send a girl out to marry the river spirit, please be sure to tell me. Tell the three elders, the priestess, and all the officials in the county that they should be there too. I wish to give her a proper send-off to her new home." Then he went off and thought about the matter for many days.

━━━━━━━━━━━━━━━━━━━━━━━━━━━━━━

Ximen Bao understood the people in the village. He recognized their deep belief in the spirits of nature and knew that he could not contradict them. What could he do to save the innocent daughters of the village without breaking the long-held traditions of the people?

Some time later, the priestess again chose a young girl to be the river spirit's bride. Ximen Bao came down to the shore to see her off, and people from all over the county came too. The three elders and other officials stood beside Ximen Bao. The priestess, an elderly woman, and her ten disciples followed close behind. Ximen Bao said, "I wish to look at the girl and see what she is like." After seeing the girl, he looked at the officials gathered before him and said, "I don't think she's pretty enough to marry the river spirit. Please ask the priestess to tell the river spirit that we'll find him a better-looking bride and send her down to him later."

With that, he instructed his own servants to throw the priestess into the river, where she sank like a stone. After a while Ximen Bao said, "She seems to be taking a long time. Let's send one of her disciples down to bring her back." One after another, Bao's men threw the priestess's disciples into the river. A few minutes later he said, "Perhaps the priestess is having a hard time explaining herself. The three elders would perhaps do better in talking with the river spirit." One by one, the three elders were thrown into the river. All the other officials trembled with fear as they watched. Bao turned and said to them, "The priestess and the three elders have not come back. What should we do now? Maybe it's time for one of you to go down and urge them to clear up the matter."

All the other officials were so afraid, they could hardly speak, but instead bowed to Ximen Bao until their foreheads knocked upon the stones on the ground. Bao said: "It seems that the river spirit is very hospitable to his guests. He keeps them for a long time. I suppose there is nothing more to do at the moment. So let us return to our work. You can all go home now."

From then on in the towns and villages of Ye County no one ever again dared to marry their young girls to the river spirit. Families returned from afar with their daughters and once again the people could farm their lands, pay their taxes, and live in peace with their neighbors and friends.

The Cloak

(Ireland)

This story belongs to the folk traditions of many areas, including the Middle East, Europe, and the Americas. It has been said that the true measure of a society is how it treats its children and its elders. The widespread appearance of this tale in the world's oral traditions shows that from ancient times until the present, people have been grappling with this important question: How do we care for our elders when they can no longer contribute to the economic well-being of the family?

Once in the city of Dublin there lived a merchant by the name of Seamus McDonnell who worked hard all his life to raise his family and provide for their welfare. He looked forward to the day when his son would take over his business, and he could rest and enjoy the fruits of all his labors. When his son was grown, Seamus told him that he was now ready to step aside. He spoke softly. "I have taught you everything you need to know. You are the head of the house now, and may it go as well for you as it did for me."

His son nodded and the two shook hands. Soon he began to manage the shipments of cloth and wool, dry goods and housewares, just as his father had taught him. But after a while, he got to thinking: "Why do I have to take care of that old man? He is of no use to anybody now, and all he does is take up a bed I could use for guests, and eat food I could use for myself."

And soon enough he had packed up a bag for his old father and sent him out into the wide world, with not so much as a thank-you for all the father had done to bring him up and raise him.

A few years went by. The son, now prospering in every way, was married and had a child of his own. One snowy evening, as he set the candles out by the window, he heard a knock on the door. When he opened it, he saw a familiar face, but the man was dressed in rags and shivering from the cold. It was his own father, Seamus McDonnell.

"I don't mean to trouble you, son," said the old man, "but I've come down on my luck, for there's nowhere for me to stay tonight." The son looked at his father, and sighed. "Well, I don't know as I have room for you, but I remember there's an old cloak of yours which we kept up in the attic. I'll bring it down, and you can take it, as you please."

The son called his own child, a little boy of seven years old, and told him, "Go up to the attic and bring down the old cloak that's hanging on the wall. It's time to give it to your grandfather."

The boy turned and went upstairs. The son waited silently by the door as the old man stood shivering and stamping his feet. A few minutes went by, the clock ticking on the mantelpiece. Then a few more. Now it was almost half an hour. The son grew impatient. "What's keeping that boy?" he muttered. "I'd better go up and see for myself."

The boy had always cared about his grandfather and wondered how he was faring. How could he use the cloak to teach his father how to treat the elder Seamus McDonnell?

When the son went upstairs into the dusty attic, he found his little boy sitting on the floor, carefully cutting the cloak with a great pair of shears. "What are you doing!" roared his father. "What are you wasting time for up here and why are you cutting that good cloth with your mother's favorite shears?"

The boy looked up. "Why, Father," he said, "I'm cutting the cloak in half so I'll have something left when I send you out of the house and you come knocking at the door."

· · · ·

Our friend Jonathan Moore, a defense lawyer, once had to represent the claims of a man who was fired after many years of serving his company, just before he was about to receive his pension. Jon said this was the kind of story he could use to help sway the jury on his client's behalf. If the company could fire this man, who is to say that members of the next generation would have protection when it was their turn to retire?

Bringing Wrongdoers to Justice: Matters of Guilt and Innocence

Before a criminal can be brought to justice, his or her wrongdoing must be exposed. In the American system, the accused are "innocent until proven guilty," and they must be proven guilty beyond a reasonable doubt. In these stories, heroes use their wits to expose wrongdoings and bring the criminals to justice. Care to match wits with them?

The Thief and the Pig

(China)

Stories of judges appear often in Chinese folklore. One of the most famous judges is Pao Cheng (999– 1062 C.E.), who lived during the Ming dynasty (960–1279 C.E.). Pao Cheng was an administrator of the imperial court in Peking. Because Pao was so greatly respected for his wisdom, the emperor sent him to travel throughout the land to determine if laws were being carried out correctly and if justice and order prevailed. This story is said to be based on an actual event that was recorded during the Qing dynasty (1644–1911).

Once in Guangdong Province, in South China, in a small and remote village, a farmer raised a pig. When the pig was grown, it weighed almost 130 pounds. The farmer knew he would be able to make a good sale and bring new sacks of seeds, cloth, and a few extra coins back to his family. One night, he rubbed the pig till his coat shone, and cleaned the pig's stall for the last time. Then he went to bed, knowing that in the morning he would be taking his prize livestock to market.

In the morning, he heard his son calling out to him, "Father! Father! The stall is empty! Someone has stolen our pig!" The farmer rushed outside and sure enough, the stall was empty, with only a bucket of water left standing in the open door. Just then, a neighbor walked by. "What's all the commotion about?" he asked. When he heard what had happened, he cocked his head to one side and said, "Hmm . . ." And he described what he had seen, pointing his finger toward a neighboring village. "If you go down the road and look for a short, round-faced man, I think he could tell you something about where your pig is. I saw him bring a bucket of water and slops to his farm, and I know he's never owned a pig before!"

The farmer ran down the road to the next village. As he turned a corner, he bumped into a short man with round, puffy cheeks. He grabbed him and accused him of stealing his prize pig. But the man denied everything. "Why should I steal your pig? Who would believe such a story? You have no proof!"

So the farmer brought him before the judge. The judge asked the accused man if he knew anything about the theft of the pig. The man puffed up his cheeks till they were even rounder than before and said, "Your Honor, what would I know about a pig? If I were to steal his pig, I would have to go in the dark of night, stepping over stones all along the way. I would have to find my way to the pig's stall without waking a soul, and cover the animal in a sack made of hemp. And look at me—I'm short enough as it is. That pig must be heavy. How could I carry such an animal?"

———————————————————————

The judge thought the matter over. He suspected the short man of the crime, but there had been no witnesses. How could he prove that the man was capable of such an act, and that he was indeed guilty of the crime?

"You are right," the judge said finally. "I have thought the matter over, and decided that this farmer is accusing you without just cause. The court will give you ten thousand coins in compensation for the damage done to your name and reputation." And he ordered his assistant to go to the treasury and bring back huge strings of coins and put them in a bag. When the bag was full, and the money all counted, the judge sent the short man on his way. The man picked up the sack, put it on his back, and began to walk out of the court, thinking, "What fools these judges are!" But before he reached the door, the judge ordered him to stop.

"So, my friend, for a short man, you somehow have the strength to carry a huge sack of coins, 130 pounds' worth, in fact. I didn't ask you how to steal a pig, yet you gave me a detailed description, and you do have the strength to carry out the job!" The short man let go of the bag of coins and it fell to the ground with a crash. He confessed his crime and begged for a merciful sentence. The judge ordered that he return the pig and spend two nights in prison.

That day, the farmer drove his pig in front of him, all the way to the market, and came home with a new bag of seeds, some yards of cloth, and ten bags of coins—which kept him and his family well fed all that year and the next one too.

The Testimony of the Fly

(V i e t n a m)

Vietnam is a country of monsoon rains and rice paddies, bordered by China to the north, Laos and Cambodia to the west, and the South China Sea to the east. The country has a diverse geography of low-lying plains, seacoast, and mountain chains. The rich deltas of the Red River are to the north and the Mekong River runs to the south. In Vietnam, a continuous culture has flourished since the founding of the Hong Bang dynasty in 2897 B.C.E. Despite wars, invasions, and influences by foreign regimes—from China (since at least 111 B.C.E.) to French and American rule in the twentieth century—the Vietnamese people have maintained a rich body of music, ritual, lore, and legend that is unique to their language, culture, and history. This story from the oral tradition is retold from the collection of Mai Vo-Dinh, in his book The Toad Is the Emperor's Uncle: Animal Tales from Vietnam. *Mr. Vo-Dinh heard this and other stories while growing up in Vietnam, in the city of Hue.*

O nce in Vietnam there was a farmer who worked hard to grow his crops and feed his family. But one year, during a drought, he had no rice and no savings left. He went to Tung Nguyen, the village moneylender, and asked if he could borrow a sum of money, saying that he would pay him back at the next harvest. The moneylender told him that if he didn't repay the loan by then, the farmer would have to forfeit his farm and give everything to him. The farmer had no choice. To survive this season, he had to agree. And so Tung Nguyen gave him the sum he needed. He grumbled when he handed over the coins, but secretly he was glad. Tung was sure that now he would have another piece of property to own, as he had gained others before. By this time, the moneylender was so well off, he didn't have to work at all—but he was always looking for more to own.

The farmer worked as hard as he could. His wife and small son helped him. After the drought, their harvest improved, but they certainly did not have enough to pay back all that they owed to the money-lender. The date of payment was approaching. One morning, the farmer and his wife set out to see what they could do to earn some money. They left their son, a little boy of eight years old, to watch the farm.

A little while later, Tung Nguyen, impatient to make his demands and take the farm, walked through the front gate. The farmer and his wife were nowhere to be seen, but the small boy was sitting there, playing with stones. "Ahem," said the moneylender. "Where are your parents? I've come to collect my debt."

The small boy looked up. "Oh, my parents aren't here."

"Where are they, then?"

"My father has gone to cut live trees and plant dead ones, and my mother has gone to sell the wind and buy the moon."

Tung Nguyen stopped in his tracks. "What do you mean by those words?" But the boy only looked up and slowly repeated them. The moneylender shook the bamboo stick he was carrying in the boy's face. "You had better tell me what you mean, or there will be trouble for you!"

The boy only repeated the phrase again, till finally the moneylender said, "I must know what you mean by those words! Tell me now—let heaven and earth be my witness—and I will cancel the debt your father owes me!"

The boy looked up.

"All of it?"

"All of it!" said Tung.

"But sir, heaven and earth cannot speak, they cannot bear witness. I will tell you, if only you let a living thing bear witness."

The moneylender was getting impatient, and besides, he had no intention of keeping his promise. A fly was buzzing nearby and lighted on his bamboo stick. "Very well, let the fly be our witness. And now, will you tell me what you mean by cutting down live trees and planting dead ones, and selling the wind to buy the moon?"

The boy stared for a moment at the fly as it calmly rested on top of the bamboo pole. "Very well, a fly is as good a witness as any. I will tell you now what I mean, since I know you will keep your promise. My father went to cut down trees and make a fence with them for a neighbor, so he could earn some money to help pay our debt. Didn't he cut down live trees and plant dead ones? My mother went to sell fans so that she could buy oil for our lamps. Isn't that selling the wind to buy the moon?"

The rich man shook his head and left, thinking that the boy was a clever one—and too bad that in a few days he would be homeless. The next day, he came back, and this time the farmer and his wife were there. He demanded his payment. The farmer begged for a delay. The moneylender refused. Hearing the argument, the little boy rushed up and said, "Father, Father, you don't have to pay anymore! Tung Nguyen promised he would cancel all of our debts."

Of course the moneylender denied ever having said such a thing, but the boy insisted. There was nothing to do but bring the matter before a mandarin scholar, the town judge.

The judge listened to what each had to say. Then he turned to the boy. "You say that the moneylender promised he would cancel the debt, but how do we

know you didn't just make the whole story up? You have no witnesses to prove it!"

"Your Honor," said the boy, "there *was* a witness. It was a fly."

"A fly!" roared the judge. "What are you talking about? Even from a child, we won't tolerate nonsense in this court."

The judge was right. There were no witnesses. What could the boy say about the fly to prove his story was true?

The boy looked at his parents, then turned again to face the judge, speaking every word with a clear voice. "Yes, there was a fly," said the child. "He was there the whole time, sitting on the moneylender's nose."

"Why, that's ridiculous!" Tung Nguyen said as he jumped up. "That fly wasn't sitting on my nose. He was sitting on my bamboo pole—"

But he stopped himself before saying another word. For, of course, now he had confessed everything.

The mandarin laughed. "Sometimes," he said,

"even the smallest creature can bear witness, but it takes a child to prove it! The court rules that you must cancel your debt, as you promised." And so the farmer and his wife returned home with their son. They lived there and prospered for many years. And when the boy grew up and had his own children, he told them that the farm would be theirs too—all because of the testimony of a fly.

Susannah and the Elders

(Ancient Israel)

The Ten Commandments have been a guidepost for many people since they were first written down in the Torah, also known as the Five Books of Moses. Biblical scholars have noted a connection between the laws of Moses and earlier sets of laws from the Middle East, such as Hammurabi's code from Mesopotamia. The Apocrypha were a selection of stories not included in the collection of texts that became the Torah. However, they were still considered by scribes of the time to have value as sacred books, and so they were preserved and passed on. The story of "Susannah and the Elders," a late addition to the Book of Daniel, focuses on the ninth commandment, "Thou shall not bear false witness."

Once in ancient Israel there was a man named Chelcias, whose daughter Susannah was known for her beauty and the righteousness of her ways. Susannah was married to a man named Joakim. He had a house and a fragrant garden. People loved to come to the house and especially to sit in his garden. Susannah always welcomed them and treated people with kindness and hospitality. But one day, two elders, men who were appointed as judges over the village, came to the house of Joakim. They had heard of his garden, but more than that, they wished to visit with Susannah, for they had heard of her kindness and beauty.

Every day they spent in the garden, and whenever Susannah passed by or spoke a word to them, their hearts beat fast. Each of the elders wanted to speak to her. Each of them wanted her to leave her husband and go with him. One day they decided to draw Susannah into a trap. They watched and waited until she went into her own corner of the garden, which was locked behind a wooden gate. They knew that day that Susannah was going to bathe. After she sent her servants away, the elders opened the gate themselves, and found her standing near a pool of clear water. She was frightened when she saw them, and drew a linen cloth tightly around her.

"What do you want?" she said. "This is no place for you!"

The two elders stood beside her. "Susannah," they said, "both of us want to take you away. Come away with us now, and leave your husband. If you don't do as we say, we will tell everyone that a young man was here with you today, embracing you, and you will be disgraced before the people and sentenced to death."

Susannah was afraid. She knew that these were powerful men who could do her great harm if she refused. But her heart was strong, and finally she spoke to them and said, "If I disobey you, you may shame me before my family and friends. You may even sentence me to death. But if I follow you and leave my husband, then I will have betrayed not only my family but the laws of God. I will hear no more from you. Do what you must."

The two elders were insulted by her words. Immediately they made an outcry and called the servants. "Susannah was here with a young man, a stranger to our village. We saw them embracing under a tree in the garden. Now we will bring judgment upon her."

The next day, Susannah was brought before the court. Her family and husband stood near her, weeping. Even in her disgrace, with head bowed, she shone with an inner light of beauty. The elders brought their case against her, and none could speak against them—for who could contradict them? There were no other witnesses. The elders used the force of law against her, and sentenced her to death.

Hearing their words, Susannah looked up into the bright sky above her. "O Lord," she cried out. "You know the secrets of the hearts of all people. But behold, now I must die for what these two have said against me in the hardness of their hearts!"

Suddenly there appeared in the crowd a young man. His eyes shone with a burning fire, and he spoke in a voice that sounded as strong and true as the blast of a trumpet. "You are fools, you sons of Israel, that have condemned her to death without examination or knowledge of the truth!"

The crowd gathered around. "But how can you prove Susannah's innocence?"

_____

The two elders could speak for each other, but no one could speak for Susannah. How could the mysterious visitor trap the two liars so that they would be forced to tell the truth?

The young man looked at the elders, who stood together, side by side, and with a quick movement he pulled them apart. He took one of them a distance from his friend and asked him, "You have said you saw Susannah embracing a young man under a tree. What kind of tree was it?"

The elder shook as he spoke. "Why, it was the eucalyptus tree, of course."

And the people listened.

Then the young man took the other elder aside and said, "You say that you have seen Susannah with a young man under a tree. Can you name the tree?" The elder shook in his shoes. "Of course, it was the palm tree!"

"Thou shalt not bear false witness against thy neighbor!" said the young man. "Thus has the Lord commanded. But your own words have proven that your accusations are lies and that Susannah is blameless." The people shouted in agreement. And that day, justice was served according to the ancient laws of Israel, and the two elders were put to death. Susannah returned with her husband to their home, and the people rejoiced in the honor and innocence of their friend and neighbor. As the evening sun shed its light on the garden, Susannah looked up and saw the young man, his eyes glowing now with the radiance of the sun. "Tell me your name," she said. "How can I remember you?"

"I have many names," he said, "but you can call me Daniel, the judge of the Lord."

"Daniel," she said in thanks, as he walked out the gate. She watched until she could see him no more, until even his shadow had faded, swallowed up in the darkening horizon of the evening sky.

The Jury

(United States)

"A right to a trial by jury," says Justice Eugene Pincham, "is one of the most precious of all human rights." As a young black man, he was fully aware of the history of slaves and their descendants, many of whom were lynched without ever going to trial. In his personal quest for justice, Eugene Pincham became a lawyer, then a judge in Chicago. He told Steve about the bright moment in human history when the jury trial became part of Western tradition.

King John I, he explained, was one of the worst kings England ever had. Wreaking havoc on England in the thirteenth century, his actions infuriated the bishops and barons in his kingdom. He stole money and property from the church. He forced merchants in his kingdom to share their profits with him—if they refused, he put them out of business or in jail without a trial.

In King John's day, and throughout England's history, justice was dispensed by judges appointed

*directly by the king. The citizens had no say.
Judges were beholden to the crown. They generally
determined a person's guilt by considering whether
or not their employer—the king—wanted that
person found guilty.*

*When the barons of his kingdom could no
longer tolerate the king's abuses, they approached
the king with an inspired list of demands. On June
15, 1215, on a meadow called Runnymede, on
the Thames River, the Magna Carta (or Great
Charter) was signed into law by King John of
England. It was the first time in Western history
that a king was forced to acknowledge that his
subjects had rights, human rights. Among the pro-
visions of the charter was a person's right to be
judged by a jury of his peers, his equals:*

We will deny no man justice. No man shall
be taken or imprisoned . . . except by a jury
of his peers.

*These words were an inspiration for Eugene Pin-
cham. He went on to spend twenty-five years as a
lawyer advocating for his clients' defense. He then
spent twenty years as a judge, presiding over the*

*court. "But I have an abiding respect for juries,"
Justice Pincham said. "This is a story that is part
fact and part fiction. I tell it to show how astute
the members of a jury can be."*

I n a county outside of Chicago, I was defending a
man accused of murdering his wife. In this case
the evidence against my client was circumstantial.
That is, there were no eyewitnesses and no absolute
proof. His wife was missing, and a few weeks before her disappearance, my client had taken out a
million-dollar insurance policy on her. The policy
was written in such a way that it paid double if she
suffered a violent death or disappearance. At the
murder trial, witnesses for the prosecution testified
to my client's violent behavior, and some said that
they had seen him strike his wife in anger in the
months leading up to her disappearance. But that's
about all they had on him.

In closing arguments, I passionately argued my
case to the jury. "You can't deny a man the precious,
God-given right of freedom based upon this kind of
meager evidence. To prove a case, it is necessary to
preclude and exclude every reasonable hypothesis.

THE COW OF NO COLOR · 50

In our system, you have to prove a man guilty beyond a reasonable doubt.

"The prosecutor really doesn't have a case. The fact of the matter is he hasn't even proven beyond a reasonable doubt that the defendant's wife is dead, let alone that my client killed her or caused her disappearance."

Then I said, "Ladies and gentlemen of the jury, I don't think you are even convinced that my client's wife is *dead*. As a matter of fact," I said, and at that moment I pointed to the door of the courtroom, "there's his wife walking in the door right now!"

And all the jurors looked at the door.

"You see! The fact that you looked at the door clearly demonstrates that you don't believe my client's wife is really dead." I sat down, in victory, knowing that I had won this case.

The jury went out and deliberated five minutes. The foreman and the members of the jury returned to the courtroom. The judge asked for the verdict. I couldn't believe it. They found my client guilty of murder.

At that point I just put my head in my hands. I was not accustomed to losing cases. Then, when the court adjourned, I found the foreman of the jury and asked him, "How could you possibly have found my client guilty? You couldn't have been convinced that he killed his wife. You weren't even convinced his wife was dead! When I said, 'Look, she's walking in the door,' all twelve of you turned your heads."

Can you guess why the jury found my client guilty?

The foreman of the jury looked at me and said, "That's right, when you told us that his wife was walking into the court, all twelve of us looked at the door. But your client didn't even turn his head. He knew she couldn't be there."

Although I lost the case, I tell the story because it demonstrates the astuteness and sophistication of the jury.

❯❯❮❯❯❮❯❮❯❮❯ Forgiveness and Mercy: Throwing the First Stone

As Rabbi Edward Schecter put it, "Justice is what we want for the other guy. Mercy is what we want for ourselves." Forgiveness and mercy are part of our system of justice. A piece of wisdom from the Jewish tradition asks, "What would the world be like if there were only justice and no mercy?" Can you think what would happen?

If in this world there were only justice, an unemployed father who stole some medicine for his dying daughter would be put to death. The world would be filled with stories like that. But what if there were only mercy and no justice? Then a person who killed his neighbor for stealing a piece of fruit from his tree—or who killed *you* for no reason—would go free!

The world needs both justice and mercy to ensure fairness. There is even an old rabbinic question that asks, What does God say when he prays? He says, "May my measure of justice be tempered with mercy."

These next stories pose questions about mercy and forgiveness. One asks whether a righteous person who does just one thing wrong can be forgiven; another, whether a person who does much wrong—but does just one thing right—deserves mercy.

The Magic Seed

(The Middle East)

This story can be found in many variations throughout Asia and the Middle East. Wherever it appears, the story raises the question of whether anyone is innocent enough of wrongdoing to condemn another human being to death. The story is also related to the biblical quotation from the New Testament, "He that is without sin among you, let him first cast a stone" (the Gospel of John, chapter 8, verse 7).

Once, a poor but honest man was so down on his luck that he had to steal a piece of bread from the bins behind a baker's shop to feed his family. The king's soldiers caught him as he stepped around the corner, trying to hide the bread under his tattered cloak. "The punishment for stealing is death!" they cried and brought him before the king and his grand viziers and magistrates. "The punishment for stealing is death!" They all nodded to each other, and prepared to send the man down to the dungeon to await his execution.

As the prisoner was being led away, he reached in his pocket and found a single dried pomegranate seed. Suddenly he had an idea. The man knew he had one last chance to save himself, if he could only catch the attention of the king.

"Wait," said the man. "Before I die, I'd at least like to pass on a family secret, for it would be a pity if it were lost to the world with my passing." And with that, he took the small pomegranate seed out of his pocket. The king, his viziers, and all his courtiers turned around and stared. No prisoner condemned to death had ever told them anything like that before.

How did the poor man use a seed to save his life?

The poor man told them that this seed was magical. If it were planted, it would grow and bear fruit in a single night, but only if it were planted by someone who had never told a lie, or done anything wrong, his entire life.

"To whom shall I bestow this precious seed?" he asked.

The king hemmed and hawed. He remembered once as a youth taking a jeweled penknife that didn't belong to him. The vizier trembled as he thought of other innocent men he had sent to death. He certainly couldn't take the seed. The courtiers and the soldiers all remembered something from their past. Then the poor man spoke: "I have been sentenced to death for taking a few crumbs of bread to feed my family. Yet not one of you, the great, mighty, and powerful of the land, feels you can take the seed." The king realized that the harshness of his punishment did not fit the crime and he let the poor man go.

The Bird Lovers

(L a o s)

Pakoua Vang, along with his wife and two daugh-
ters, fled the country of Laos in 1975. They are
members of the Hmong tribal communities who
sided with the United States during the war in
Vietnam. When the war was over, they had to
swim across the Mekong River in their flight from
the Communists. Their journey to safety in Thai-
land was made at night.

As Yamy Vang remembers, "It was a strenuous
and difficult journey for the family since all the
kids were under the age of ten. No one wanted to
travel with us because they were afraid that we
kids would cry out and make our hideouts known.
I remember hearing the sounds of gunfire and
grenades blowing up around us and having to be
quiet and brave. When we were afraid or scared,
my dad told us that our grandparents and ances-
tors would protect and guide us to safety."

Pakoua Vang told the story "The Bird Lovers"
to his daughter, Yamy Vang, who is now in law

school in Albany, New York. She told it to Steve in New York City. So the story has come a long way.

"The Bird Lovers" tells of a musical instrument, the xim xaus, made from a coconut, horsehair, and bamboo. The xim xaus is called a "talking instrument," because different sounds stand for certain words, so that a person can tell a story by simply bowing the strings. The instrument is often played by young men when they go courting. Sometimes a young man will propose to a woman by bowing the strings to ask if she will marry him. Yamy's father tells the story to convey values of trust, truthfulness, and forgiveness, which are very important to the Hmong people, and must be part of any system of justice.

A long time ago, there lived in the spirit world a couple called the Orphan Boy and Yer, his wife. Their love for each other was so strong that they made a solemn vow. They promised to love only each other for all eternity. Time passed, and the spirits were anxious to begin their life anew.

The Orphan Boy and Yer anxiously awaited their return to earth. The Orphan Boy was so anxious, he could barely contain himself. When their turn was called, he ran to the spirit pool and jumped into it before the beautiful Yer even reached the edge.

On the other side, the Orphan Boy emerged as an ox, and Yer came through as a mare. The two could not meet and marry. The ox was used by men to plow the rice fields, and the mare carried men's burdens. The ox was so brokenhearted that he ran to a nearby cliff, jumped off, and killed himself. Meanwhile, the mare, seeing her beloved ox dead, ran at full speed into a sharp point in a fence and killed herself. The Hmong people say that if you look at a horse's hoof and count the indentations, you can tell the number of times that the spirit who inhabits the horse has been reincarnated.

In the spirit world, Yer and the Orphan Boy waited for their chance to return. Again, the Orphan Boy was impatient, and when their turn came, he jumped into the spirit pool before Yer. He emerged on the other side as a pig. She came out on the other side as a man. Again they could not mate. The man was a farmer who took care of the pig as his pet. He was a poor man, and all he had on his farm was this fat pig. The pig could not stand to see the poor man suffering while he grew large. All the pig did all day long was eat and sit in the sun. He agonized over the suffering of the farmer and came to a conclusion: I must begin anew.

Seeing a sharp edge on the fence, the pig ran right into it, killing himself. Heartbroken over the death of the pig, the farmer died of loneliness.

In the spirit world, the Orphan Boy and his wife once again awaited their turn at the spirit pool. This time they realized that when they failed to wait for each other, they turned into different species. They decided to jump into the pool holding hands. This time, they emerged as a bird couple.

The birds were happy and cheerful, chirping all day long, and building their nest and their new home in a tree rooted in a broad field of grain. Soon they were expecting babies. Yer watched over the eggs, and her husband flew far and wide to find twigs and leaves to build their nest.

On his travels, he noticed that men were beginning to get their soil ready for planting. He watched with horror as they built a raging fire to clear the land. He told his wife about the fire approaching their nest. As he spoke, the savage flames sizzled along the underbrush, racing toward the tree. He asked Yer, "Should we stay with our eggs, our chil-

dren, or should we leave our children behind to start our life anew?" The wife replied, "No, it has taken us this long to start a family, and we should all stay together whether we live or we die." The husband told her, "You lay over our eggs, and I will protect you from the treetop."

By the time he reached the top, he could feel the burning heat. When he returned to the nest it appeared as if the flames were going to eat him alive. He feared for his life, and in a deep panic flew out of the nest. Yer, her head bent over her babies, did not even see the fire. She died with her children in the nest. Her husband wandered the world until he died.

Many lifetimes later, in a southern village there lived a lovely, talented, and beautiful young lady who spoke not one word. Her beauty was compared to the moon and the sun, and her skills and her stitchery to the artistry of termites, who carve fine channels as they travel through wood. She also was compared to the ants for her hard work and responsibility and loyalty to her family.

Her father was the rich village chief. Concerned about his daughter's strange silence, he announced to the world that anyone who could get his daughter to speak would be awarded her hand in marriage.

A prince in a northern region heard of this announcement and made preparations to go south. He told his followers and his people that the princess would speak to him when she viewed his beautiful face. He said, "Who can refuse me? I am handsome, I am strong, I am rich. I am powerful, and I am a prince."

Among his followers was a gentle soul known as the Poor Man, who had grown up as an orphan child. The Poor Man heard about the prince's plan to travel south to marry the young woman. He was curious about this beautiful woman and decided to follow. He was pulled by a force he did not fully understand.

On his way south, he saw a coconut on the roadside and picked it up. He drank the coconut milk and decided to keep the shell. Many days later, he noticed a bamboo stick. He picked it up. "You never know when you might need it," he said, and placed it beside the coconut in his sack.

As he approached the village, he saw a long line of splendidly dressed young suitors talking excitedly about their skills and their abilities and their plans to court the young lady. He saw the prince go up to the head of the line and push all the other young men aside. The prince approached the young woman, whose name was . . . Yer. "Yes, indeed, it is her!" thought the Poor Man. She was the lovely wife of his former lifetimes.

The prince talked to her, composing poetry off the top of his head. He sang and he danced. He tried to cajole her. He posed in all his splendor in many positions, hoping that she would look at him and speak. But she did not. He told his followers to display the gifts he had brought. They brought rolls of silk in many colors, along with incense and jewels. She looked at all of his riches and said not one word. Her father, chief of this southern village, told the prince to sit down and let the other young men try.

All the young men took their turns, trying to tease the beautiful lady and to make her laugh. They sang to her, and they composed poetry in honor of her beauty and her skill. But Yer said not one word.

As the sun was setting, the silent girl's father told all the young men to go take a rest. At the end of the line, the father saw the Poor Man sitting in a corner, patiently awaiting his turn. The prince said, "Chief, you do not want that Poor Man; he is not worthy of your daughter. Look at him, see his pants, they only reach to his knee, and his shirt only to his elbow. Look at his bare feet and the dirt under his fingernails."

"You have had your turn, Prince," said the chief. "Now take a seat. I am a fair man. Every suitor must have his chance."

The Poor Man approached Yer. With a bow of horsehair, he began to play his instrument, made of a coconut and bamboo. The *xim xaus* spoke as a human voice would speak, telling the story of the bird couple, how they built their nest in a tree in the field. Suddenly, the princess winced as she recognized this bedraggled suitor. The notes of the *xim xaus* told of a fire approaching and of a bird asking his wife, "Should we stay with our children or should we fly away?" The notes told of the wife's reply, "We should stay."

After so many years of repeating the cycles of life and death, the Poor Man felt he had one last

*chance to say something that would bring them fi-
nally together. What could he say that would get
her to speak and become his bride?*

The *xim xaus* told of how the wife looked up and
saw the fire. In a panic, *she* flew from the nest in fear
of her life, leaving her husband and her children to
die.

At this point, Yer, who all day and all week had
been sitting patiently through the courtships, stood
up and hit the table, shouting, "It was you, not me!
You betrayed me! I didn't leave you. You left me to
die!"

The Poor Man approached Yer, got down on his
knees, and begged her forgiveness. He explained to
her that he had wanted to stay, but did not realize
how frightening the fire was going to be. He admitted that he was afraid, a coward, when he flew from
the nest without her.

———————————————————————

If you were the princess, would you take him back?

• • • •

The princess simply smiled. Her father, seeing his daughter's joy, took the hand of the princess and placed it in the Poor Man's hand. "You have my daughter now; she is your wife. I give you her hand in marriage. You must remember, young man, to keep your promises. Look what happened—I, her father, have been denied the sound of her voice for these many years because of your betrayal. But a person's whole life should not be ruined because of a single moment of fear. To be truly fair, justice must include forgiveness and mercy."

An Ounce of Mud

(Eastern Europe)

This story from Jewish folklore centers on the belief in a higher justice that all human beings must account to—if not in this life, then in the hereafter. It also relates to the idea in other religions, such as the Hindu and Buddhist concept of Karma, that how we act in this life can have a profound effect on events in the future.

R eb Nachum was a man who had always done well for himself. But he never had time to give a hand to others. You could never be sure if a trade with him was everything it should be, as he always seemed to walk away with a little more than was originally called for in the bargain. His wife and children he rarely saw, and when he did, it was to scold them for something they hadn't done right. He spent a lot of time running around the countryside, earning as much as he could, and rarely if ever was a guest invited to his house for the Sabbath.

One evening, he was traveling in his coach down a dark country road. It was almost sundown and the Sabbath was near. All of a sudden he heard a neighing sound and someone calling out for help. He stopped his carriage. There, by the roadside, was a poor peasant, a Jew whose horse was sinking into a mud hole and the wagon going down fast with it. The peasant was pulling with all his might, but it looked as if both the horse and wagon would be lost.

Without thinking, Reb Nachum called his coachman to come and help. They tied the horse's bridle to the back of his carriage, and the two of them got behind the wagon and pushed. With the peasant pulling from his end, the horse was freed and the wagon dragged up out of the mud. "Thank you, friend. Had it not been for you, I would have lost my horse and wagon, and been late for the Sabbath besides." Reb Nachum nodded and brushed some mud off the peasant's shoulders.

"There, you look ready to go now!" And they said farewell.

Reb Nachum soon forgot all about this incident. He had so many schemes to invent and carry out. He ended up amassing great wealth, but most of it came through tricks or deceit. His wife and children he left to fend for themselves. By the end of his life, not much good could be said of him, and rich though he was, only a few came to his funeral.

Up in heaven, Reb Nachum stood before the Divine Court. The scales stood on the gleaming golden table. The Prosecuting Angel stood on one side, and read down the record of Reb Nachum's life: the time he cheated the baker, the times he spoke harshly to his children, the years he spent amassing all his money and never thinking to give any to the poor or needy. The scale had sunk all the way to the prosecution's side. The angel said, "We see nothing here to recommend Reb Nachum. His place is not in heaven!"

As the Defending Angel looked back over Reb Nachum's past in desperation, he could identify only one good deed. So he placed the poor man's wagon on the scales. Miraculously, the scales held in perfect balance for a brief moment, but then they started to tip back to the prosecution's side. The Defending Angel let out a deep sigh.

Was there anything else the Defending Angel could place on the scales that would sway them in favor of Reb Nachum? How would you defend him—if you had to?

The Defending Angel scoured the pages. "Wait," the angel said, "I think I have something here." He reached out and put something on the scales. Slowly, slowly the scales began to move in the other direction. The angels gathered around to see. It was the ounce of mud that Reb Nachum had brushed off the coat of the peasant, and it tipped the scales in his favor.

❯❯❯❯❯❯❯ Settling Disputes: Between a Rock and a Hard Place

Justice often comes down to tough choices. In these stories, you will have to decide who will live and who will die, who will be jailed and who will go free, who will be honored and who will be shunned. Sometimes, settling a dispute comes down to showing opposing sides that they are not as far apart as they think they are. Other times, a story can tell us that there is no one "right" answer but that to come to the best decision, everybody's point of view needs to be heard and considered.

The Dance of Elegba

(Nigeria, Cuba)

In the West African Yoruba tradition there are many deities, called orishas, which represent forces of nature and aspects of the universe both human and divine. The god Elegba is the deity of the crossroads, the messenger between heaven and earth. He has many aspects and many different roles to fulfill. Often he appears as a trickster. He can cause confusion, but he can also bring clarity and understanding. Small figures or offerings to Elegba are often placed by the entrances of a household, or by the roadside, when someone is about to take a long journey. A Yoruba priest, or babalawo, *is trained to read and interpret the messages of the deities to the people in a community. Often a* babalawo *is called to help settle a dispute with his knowledge of Ifá, the system of Yoruba divination.*

This story is told not only in Nigeria, where it originated, but also in Cuba, where the lore and religion of the Yoruba people have taken root and flourished since the time of the African slave trade to the Caribbean.

——————————————————————————————————

Once there were two farmers named Olufemi and Olushegun who lived side by side in a small village outside of Ile Ife, the great Yoruba city in Nigeria. Every day they planted their crops. Every year they gathered the harvest of yams and calabash, mangoes and plantains, and brought them to the marketplace. They each had their own stall, on opposite sides of the road. But being good friends, they enjoyed passing the time together as people came by to sample their fruits or trade some cloth or a good iron tool for a basket of fresh mangoes. Olufemi and Olushegun always made their decisions together.

Whether it was picking the right way to plant their crops, or finding the best day to start a journey, or judging how to discipline their sons and daughters, they would make sure to consult with each other. And they always agreed. "How wise my friend Olufemi is," Olushegun, nodding, would say. "I agree with Olushegun," said his friend, "because he is always right." And they vowed never to fight.

One day, Elegba, the orisha of chance and deity of the crossroads, looked upon these two friends. "Their lives go well and they prosper," he said, "but life does not go in a straight line. Sometimes there are zigzags. Life without contradictions is not the destiny of human beings. These two must come to know the meaning of my powers, given to me by Olorun, creator of all the deities and of the world itself, or their friendship is nothing but a hollow reed and not the strong tree they can truly depend on."

Market day came. Olufemi and Olushegun traveled together to their spot by the road to sell produce and meet their friends and neighbors as usual. That day, Elegba, messenger of fate, deity of chance and accident, prepared himself for his visit. He dressed himself in his many-colored cloth, and picked up his staff. He spun around and put a hat on his head. One side of the hat was red, the other black. Small cowry shells hung around the edges of the hat and jingled as he walked.

Elegba strolled down the road to the marketplace until he saw the two farmers talking, one to the other, from across the road. Dancing a little dance, and singing a song, he passed between them, tapping his wooden staff on the ground. After he had

gone by, Olufemi said to his friend, "Did you see the fellow who just passed by? I liked his song, but what about that black hat he was wearing? I've never seen one like it."

Olushegun looked at his friend. "Oh, I saw that man pass. I liked his song too, but he was wearing a red hat, so you must have seen a different fellow."

Olufemi stared at his friend. "I can tell you, he just walked by, he was singing and tapping his stick, and his hat was black as the tar on my gum tree."

"My friend, I do not like to contradict you, but you are entirely wrong, because the hat he was wearing was red as the berries I'm selling from my basket."

Olufemi stepped away from his wares and walked to the middle of the road. "You really must be seeing things," he said, "because the hat was black." Olushegun stepped onto the road. "Are you telling me I'm wrong? That hat was red, red, and only red!" and he tapped his friend on the shoulder. "Do you get my point?"

"Oh, I get your point," said Olufemi. "The man with the black hat—I saw him, and there's no doubt about it, so take that!" and he pushed his friend back a little harder.

"It was red!" "No, it was black!" "Red!" "No, black!" Back and forth, they pushed and shoved until before you know it, the two of them were rolling in the dust of the road, pummeling each other with their fists.

A crowd gathered around them and tried to pull them apart, but things just kept getting worse. Olufemi was pulling at the shoulder cloth Olushegun wore. Olushegun was kicking Olufemi in the shins with all his might, and each was yelling at the top of his lungs. "It was a black hat!" "No, it was a red hat!" "You are a liar!" "No, you are the liar here!"

The two farmers had always been good friends. Now they had come to blows. Elegba, master of fate and chance, had caused the confusion. What could he do, in his role as Divine Messenger of Justice, to show the farmers the source of their misunderstanding?

The fight continued, but suddenly, the crowd heard someone coming down the road singing a song. The song got louder and louder, and even as the fight was raging, people turned to hear it. Suddenly an old man burst through the crowd and stood before Olufemi and Olushegun.

"See, my friends—for all these years you have worked together and lived as brothers. Now you are willing to break your friendship, but before you do, watch what I have to show you!"

And very slowly, the old man began to spin. First the black side of the hat appeared. Then the red side. Olufemi sat up. He forgot all about fighting with Olushegun when he saw the dancer spinning before him. Olushegun sat up and stared as the old man, with the lightness and grace of a youth, spun around, faster and faster, till soon he could see only a whirl of colors: black and red, black and red, black and red, black and red. Then, in an instant, the dancer was gone.

The crowd parted. Olufemi stood up and held out his hand to Olushegun. "My friend," he said, "what a mistake was made here. I was only seeing one side, and that was mine."

Olushegun smoothed the dust off his friend's shoulder cloth. "I too, my friend, was only seeing one side, from my side of the road. Now we know always to look at both sides of the dancer before we decide what color hat he is wearing!"

They finished selling their goods and then set off down the road together. Before they entered their homes, they made sure to leave a special offering to the shrine of Elegba, who showed them to look one step beyond their own place on the road before losing a friend, or a good day of work at the marketplace of Ile Ife.

The Three Wives of Nenpetro

(Central Africa)

In American courts, lawyers argue points of law to prove to a jury that their client's side of the case is right. One way or the other, the jury must come up with a decision. But what if there is no "right decision"? When jurors cannot agree, the case must be tried over again. In the oral traditions of some African peoples, stories called "dilemma tales" are posed to the listeners. These stories do not have one right answer; rather, they are told to provoke discussions. Every person's interpretation is heard, but usually the opinion of the person who speaks most clearly and with the deepest knowledge of tradition and custom is respected the most. Here is a dilemma tale from the African tradition for you to think and talk about.

The Bakongo people live throughout the areas of present-day Angola and the Democratic Republic of the Congo (formerly Zaire). Lubangi Muniania, an educator at the Museum of African Art in New York City, remembers hearing this story in the town of Matadi, where he lived for part of his childhood. "The stories," he explains, "are used even today to teach children a moral or lesson."

Once, in a Bakongo village in Central Africa, there lived a man named Nenpetro who had three wives. Their names were Ndoza'ntu the Dreamer, Songa'nzila the Guide, and Fulla Fulla the Raiser of the Dead. He lived with his wives in peace, for they all worked together. One day, the wives were hungry. Nenpetro went out hunting and brought down an antelope. The wives cooked and ate it, but they were still hungry. So Nenpetro went out hunting and brought back a monkey. The wives cooked and ate it, but they looked at him and held their stomachs. Nenpetro grew impatient: "Nothing will satisfy you three but an ox!" So he went far out into the bush. He saw an ox and prepared to bring it down, but before he could lift his spear, the ox charged and killed him. Now back at the village, the wives grew even hungrier than before. And they worried—where was their husband, Nenpetro? That night, they fell asleep, and Ndoza'ntu dreamed.

In the morning she awoke and told the others: "I have seen Nenpetro. He went to hunt an ox and was killed in the bush. He is lying there somewhere." Songa'nzila guided them along the paths until they found his body on the ground. Fulla Fulla went to gather herbs, and, saying special chants and prayers, she raised her husband back to life.

But now, for the first time, the three began to quarrel. Which one should their husband honor the most? "I saw him in the dream," said Ndoza'ntu. "I deserve the most honor."

"But I led us to this place," said Songa'nzila. "I deserve the most honor."

Fulla Fulla said, "I brought him back to life. It is I who he should most honor."

As Nenpetro began to sit up, to breathe and talk, they said to one another, "Let us each bring him some food, and see whose he takes." The first two cooked chickens. Fulla Fulla cooked a pig. And they each brought their pots before Nenpetro.

If you were Nenpetro, which wife would you honor the most? Whose bowl of food would you take first?

Nenpetro looked around. By this time some people of the village had found their way to the spot, and they watched too. He said, "When Ndoza'ntu dreamed her dream, I could not eat the food she offered. And when Songa'nzila followed the path, I still could not sit up and eat the food. Only Fulla Fulla brought me back to life. So I will eat from her pot." And he honored Fulla Fulla by eating from her pot. Most of the people agreed and said he was right in his judgment. But some women standing by said, "No, he should have taken the food from all three and mixed them together."

What do you think?

The Flask

(Ancient Israel, Eastern Europe)

In Jewish tradition, learned rabbis often tell stories to explore questions of justice. The stories set up dilemmas that must be contemplated and evaluated in light of the wisdom and the laws found in Jewish writings. The rabbis then offer their studied opinions on the questions posed by the stories. In this story, we invite you to offer your own opinion.

A story. Two men are traveling through the desert. One of them carries a flask filled with water. The desert stretches out before them. Both men know that the closest oasis is a hundred miles away. They also know that there is only enough water to keep one man alive long enough to reach the watering hole. If the owner of the flask keeps the water for himself, he will reach the oasis alive; if he gives the flask to his companion, his friend will live and he will die; if he shares the water, both will die.

―――――――――――――――――――――――――――――

Who should drink the water?

Rabbi ben Petura, a respected Jewish thinker, argued that the water should be shared, even though both men will die. But the famous Rabbi Akiva, whose opinions generally carried the day, argued that the water should be used to save a life. He believed that the purpose of religious laws was to promote life, not to destroy it. We must choose life, he argued. If we cannot choose life for all, we must choose it for as many as possible.

Yet, if one person is to live, why should it be the man who happens to possess the water? Why not his companion? Perhaps his companion is younger, or smarter. Rabbi Akiva suggests that some objective way of choosing who will live is preferable to making a biased, personal decision as to whose life is more worthwhile. In this case, owning the flask of water is as good a reason as any for keeping it. In Jewish tradition there is a saying: "Who can say

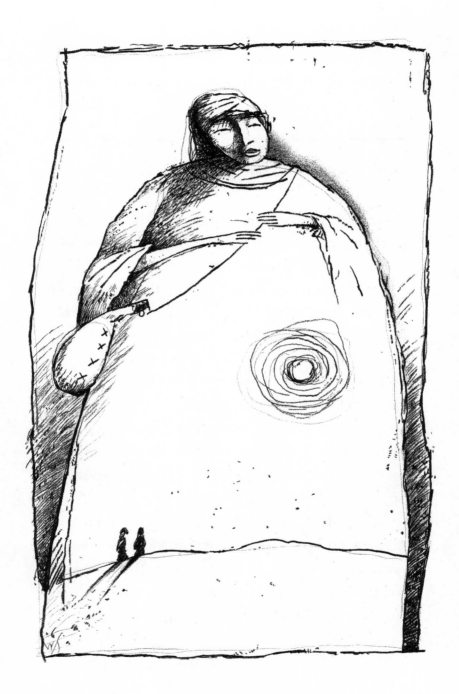

that your blood is redder than his? Who is to say
you are more worthy than he? Perhaps his blood is
redder than yours."

* * * *

Impossible situations often confront us with impossible choices. During the Holocaust—and in many
wars throughout history—mothers had to choose
between saving one or another of their children.
During the Civil War in the United States, soldiers
sometimes had to decide whether or not to kill
people from their own families who, by reason of
circumstance, fought for the opposing side. In situations like that it becomes impossible to make a just
or "best" decision. As moral human beings, we can
only work to create a world in which such horrific
choices never confront our fellow human beings or
ourselves.

⊁⊁ ⊛⊁ ⊁ ⊛⊁ ⊁ ⊛ Deciding Ownership: Who Owns the Sky?

Many Native American peoples believe that the earth is a great mother and that no one owns it. Yet the American and European system of justice is based on private property and is dedicated to figuring out just who owns what. These stories remind us that no one really owns the planet, that it is a resource here for everyone.

Kim Son Dal and the
Water-Carriers

(Korea)

Kim Son Dal was a historical figure who lived during the sixteenth century. He is known in Korean folklore as a tricky character who often uses his cleverness to help people who wouldn't otherwise be able to defend themselves against the greed or deceit of others. This story is one of the most well-known and beloved tales about Kim Son Dal. It is still told today in Korea and other parts of the world where Korean people live and work.

One day, Kim Son Dal walked by the eastern gate of the city of Pyongyang. He saw some friends of his, looking very dejected. They told him that a group of merchants from the city of Hangyang had been engaged in busy trading every day. The merchants had bought up all the rice from the nearby farms. At first, the farmers were only too

glad to sell their harvest. But soon, everyone in the
city began to suffer. The merchants now owned all
the rice, and were selling it at a price that only the
wealthy could afford. Poor people, who could not
travel to the countryside, could not pay these prices,
and many were going hungry.

Kim wanted to help his friends. He knew everybody in Pyongyang, and every nook and corner of
the city. At night he called a secret meeting of the
city's water-carriers. These were the workers who,
for just a few coins, carried water on their backs in
great clay jars from the Taedong River to the houses
of the nobles. They were among the people suffering the most from the merchants.

Kim had a bag of silver coins in his hand. He gave
a coin to each of the water-carriers and whispered
his plan in their ears. Each one would give a coin to
Kim as they passed by him on their way from the
river, and at night he would return the coins to them
so they could do it again the next day. That morning, the water-carriers did what they had promised.
As Kim sat by the eastern gate, they dropped their
coins, one by one, onto a little straw mat next to
where he was sitting. By the end of the day, he had a
large pile of coins next to him.

*How could Kim use what he knew of the mer-
chants' greed—and the coins he had gathered—to
help the water-carriers?*

Toward sunset, one of the merchants from
Hangyang walked by and noticed the sparkling silver. He stopped and stared.

"Where did you get all those silver coins from?"
the merchant asked.

Kim replied, "If you wish to know, I will tell you.
Every day, the water-carriers give me a coin as pay-
ment for the water they take from my river—the
Taedong. It's amazing how it adds up!"

The merchant couldn't believe his ears. Soon he
told all his friends and the next day they gathered
around and watched enviously as, one by one, the
water-carriers dropped their coins onto Kim Son
Dal's mat. Imagine the wealth they could acquire
with those piles of coins getting bigger and bigger
every day! A hundred times more than the baskets
of rice they sold!

Finally they could hold back no longer. They had
to strike a bargain with him. The merchants begged

Kim to come with them to an inn where they could sit and talk the matter over. They were sure that with the payment from the water-carriers, they would soon amass even greater fortunes themselves.

At first Kim was reluctant to sell. "I've made a good living from that river," he said. "I'd hate to give it up."

The merchants offered him one price after another, but he refused, until, finally, they put together all their earnings from their stay in Pyongyang—about three thousand gold coins. With a sigh, he agreed and sold them the rights to the river.

The merchants scurried away, the straw mat in hand. The next day, two of the merchants hurried to the eastern gate, where they spread out the mat and waited. Soon enough, a water-carrier walked by.

"Excuse me!" the merchants shouted. "Where's our payment?"

"Payment?" said the water-carrier. "Payment for what?"

"Why, for the water, of course. The water from the river."

"Why should I pay you?" he said. "This water

doesn't belong to anybody. It comes straight from the Taedong. You can go down there anytime and get some yourself!" And with that, he walked on.

The merchants realized soon enough that they had been tricked—and had lost all their money besides—so they gathered the last of their belongings and made their way back to Hangyang. They never came back to the Pyongyang marketplace again. As for Kim Son Dal, he distributed the price of the river—three thousand gold coins—among all the workers of the city, but especially the water-carriers. From that day he always had a friend, a meal, and a place to stay in the city of Pyongyang.

The Land

(Ancient Israel, Eastern Europe)

The Talmud is a collection of volumes that have guided the Jewish people for centuries in matters of interpreting and applying the laws of the Torah to their daily lives. The Talmud consists of arguments and opinions by various rabbis from ancient times. It also includes stories, legends, poetry, and even recipes. This is a story from the Talmud.

Once two farmers were fighting over a piece of land. Each one claimed the land belonged to him, and each one presented evidence to the other to prove his point. The first man said, "This land is mine! My grandfather planted figs here when he was a boy!" The second man said, "This land belongs to me! My grandfather and grandmother built their first home here!" They argued and argued but could come to no agreement. Finally, they decided to take their case before the town rabbi.

The rabbi listened to each of them for a long time. But even he could not decide who was right. At last, he came upon a way to discover the truth.

The rabbi took the two farmers to the field they were arguing over. As they stood there watching, he slowly bent down and put his ear to the ground.

Why did the rabbi do this? How could he help the two farmers come to a peaceful resolution of their argument by putting his ear to the ground?

The two farmers looked at each other in confusion. What did the rabbi think he was doing? He stayed there for some moments in silence. Then he stood up and looked again at the two farmers.

"My friends," he said, "I have been listening to the land, and the land has spoken. The land says it belongs to neither of you, but rather, that you belong to the land."

·   ·   ·   ·

In the Middle East, people are struggling to find a way toward peaceful coexistence. Perhaps stories like these, gathered and shared from both Jewish and Islamic traditions, could help to establish common ground. They may serve to remind us that "the land belongs to none of us, but rather that we all belong to the land."

⊷⊷⊷ Cosmic Justice: The Big Questions

Throughout human history, people have created systems of justice to bring order and fairness to life on the planet. Although many of these legal systems are flawed, they can seem quite fair when compared to the randomness of the natural world. Human beings have always wondered why nature itself does not seem fair or just. Why are so many innocent people killed, why are so many greedy people spared? Our first story comments upon a universe that is not always fair and just, at least from a human point of view.

Sharing the Soup

(M e x i c o)

In Mexico many families, even today, live close to the land and the ever turning cycles of the seasons. Before the Mexican Revolution of 1910, many of these farmers, called campesinos, *were forced to work under harsh conditions, giving up most of their produce to the owners of the sprawling ranches, called* haciendas. *Since the Spaniards arrived in the sixteenth century, the Catholic Church has been strong in Mexico, its symbols and rituals important in the countryside and city alike. In stories like this, the* campesinos *found a way to express their feelings about their lives, beliefs, and difficulties. Nina first heard this story in the late 1970s from Ken Feit, a traveling storyteller, and later from Argentina Palacios, a storyteller from Panama who lives in New York City.*

I n Mexico there once lived a peasant who worked hard all his life in the fields of a wealthy landowner. One year his crops went bad and he was soon left with the barest of scraps to eat. Finally, only a scraggly rooster running around the yard remained of all he owned. The peasant decided that he would cook the rooster and eat the soup, all by himself.

"For once," he said to himself, "I'd like to know how it feels to have a full belly!"

He caught the rooster, slaughtered it, plucked out its feathers, and put it in a pot to boil. Soon it was ready to eat. The farmer poured the soup into a bowl and was just about to taste it when he heard a knock on his door.

"Now, who could that be!" He went to open the door, and there stood San Pedro—Saint Peter— guardian of Heaven's gate, who said, "Could I share a bowl of soup with you?"

"Absolutely not!" said the peasant. "Some souls you invite into heaven. Others you send down to the flaming inferno, even for the smallest sin! No, I will not share my soup with you!" And he shut the door. He was just about to eat his soup when he heard another knock on the door. He went to open it, and this time, he saw the Blessed Virgin Mary standing there. She too wished to have a meal with him.

"Oh no, Blessed Virgin. For to some in this life you give many blessings—fortune smiles on them their whole lives—while the rest of us must live in misery and despair. No, I will not share my soup with you. Go find a meal somewhere else!" And he shut the door.

"Ah, at last I can eat my meal in peace," he said to himself. But at that moment he heard a stern knock on the door. He went to open it, and there stood the Lord. "My friend, I've been passing by and I'd like to have some of your soup! It smells delicious."

The peasant said, "I'm sorry, Lord, but no. For you are not just. Some people you create healthy and strong, yet others are lame and crippled. Some are wealthy, while others must scratch their bread every day from the hard land. No, I will not share my soup with you!" And he shut the door tight.

"Now," he said, "at last, I can finally eat my meal in peace." But just as he was about to lift the spoon to his mouth, he heard a soft tapping on the door.

"This is the last time!" he muttered. The peasant went to open the door. "Oh," he said, "it's you. You I will invite in to share this meal with me. You may come in."

The peasant had sent all his other mysterious, sacred visitors away. Yet this one he allowed into his house. Who could it have been, and why was this visitor welcomed?

The last visitor was La Muerte, Death. The peasant said, "You are just, for whether we are rich or poor, young or old, strong or weak, you come to all of us. You I will welcome into my house."

And so, the peasant and Death sat down to eat a bowl of soup together.

· · · ·

The image of death is a recurring theme in many Mexican folktales and traditions, such as the Day of the Dead, celebrated every November on All Souls' Day. On this day, families honor and remember their ancestors by visiting grave sites of departed loved ones and creating memorial altars in their homes. Children eat sugar candies in the shape of skulls, called *calevaras*, play dress-up with skeleton dolls, and eat *pan de muerto*—bread baked in the shape of bones. Children learn that death, too, is a part of life that can be confronted and even cele-brated with humor and laughter as well as tears.

A Higher Truth

(Syria)

For devout Muslims all over the world, religious beliefs and ideas about justice are defined by the holy book of the Koran, dictated by the Angel Gabriel to the Prophet Mohammad in the seventh century C.E. These themes are reflected in the folktales of the Arab world. European fairy tales often begin "Once upon a time." Arab folk stories begin with a different opening line: Kan ya ma kan, *"There was or there was not." In the rich legacy of Islamic tales, a remarkable array of folktale characters are drawn from nomadic as well as city life in desert lands. As in* The Arabian Nights, *there are stories about fishermen and clever women, poor woodcutters and talking birds, judges (qadi) and genies (djinn, invisible beings created by Allah out of smokeless fire), as well as kings and sultans who travel in disguise. This is our retelling of one such tale from Syria, first collected early in the twentieth century, and retold in Inea Bushnaq's lovely volume,* Arab Folktales.

O nce, there was or there was not a sultan who decreed that any man or woman in his king- dom who told a lie would be fined five dinars. He sent his town crier up and down the winding streets and crooked byways of the land. "Anyone who lies is subject to stiff fines," the crier announced. Then the sultan and his *wazir* (minister) disguised them- selves, and traveled those same streets to enforce the law, and keep the kingdom honest.

Their very first stop was at the home of the wealthiest merchant in all the kingdom. He invited them to his home, and made them comfortable with coffee and dried figs. Getting right to the point, they tested the merchant with pointed questions. "How old are you?" the sultan probed.

"Thanks be to Allah, I've had twenty good years," the merchant replied.

"How many sons do you have?"

"I have one single, praiseworthy son," he said.

"How much wealth have you accumulated?"

"Seventy thousand dinars, for Allah's sake," he answered.

The sultan thanked the merchant for his honesty, and returned to the palace. As they checked the town records the next day, the two men could barely contain their glee. They had caught the merchant lying. The sultan's *wazir* approached the merchant with two of his soldiers and ordered him to come to the palace. The sultan sat at the head of the palace court, where he presided over a group of judges in the royal tribunal. Again, he minced no words.

"You told us you were twenty years old," the sultan said, "but the court records show that you are seventy-five. You told us you have accumulated only seventy thousand dinars, but you have more wealth than any man in our kingdom. And you told us that you have but one son; the court records show that you have six. We hereby order you to pay a fine of fifteen dinars and spend the night in jail."

"Hear me out," said the merchant. "By Allah's word, I have told you the truth."

———————————————————————————

How could the merchant be telling the truth, when all that he said contradicted the records of the town?

"You asked how old I am," the merchant said. "I answered that I have had twenty good years—for my first twenty years were happy ones. You asked how many sons I have. I told you I have only one because the remaining five are drunkards. My single blessed son is the only one who worships Allah and brings me joy. And you asked about my wealth. I spent seventy thousand dinars to build the town mosque. That is the only treasure that matters to me, praised be Allah."

For a moment, the sultan was silent. Then, softly, he admitted, "There is no time worthy of remembrance that was not spent in happiness; no son is worth mentioning except he who is faithful and blessed; and no wealth is worth counting that was not dedicated to Allah, of blessed fame. The merchant is right: There is a more personal and sacred way to figure time, calculate wealth, and recognize those close to our hearts. We try to judge the truth in a court of men. But there is a higher truth and a higher form of justice than we may ever know."

The Walnut and the Pumpkin

(India)

This brief tale is from the state of Kashmir in northern India, on the border with Tibet. More than a thousand languages are spoken in India, but most of the population speaks one of fifteen different native languages. Kashmiri is spoken by over two million people. Stories travel back and forth between peoples in India. According to A. K. Ramanujan, who gathered this tale for his collection Folktales from India, *this story is also told in the Punjabi language, as well as in Swedish, Spanish, Hungarian, and English.*

———————————————————————

O nce there lived a man who was dissatisfied with the world. He felt that he lived on a planet presided over by a God who was neither wise nor just. One day he was sitting beneath a walnut tree when he spied a large pumpkin growing nearby. "Dear God," said this dissatisfied soul to his Maker, "how foolish you are! To create a tiny wal-

nut, you create a powerful tall tree, but to grow a pumpkin, you make only a bush with vines. How senseless can you be—to give such small nuts to such a large tree, and so large a fruit to a mere plant!"

Just then he was startled by a walnut that fell from the tree and landed with a sting on his head.

———————————————————————————

Suddenly, he became acutely aware of God's justice and wisdom. What changed his mind?

"Dear God," he exclaimed, "I am thankful to you. If you had placed your pumpkins on a walnut tree, I'd be dead right now. Great is your justice, your goodness, and your wisdom!"

►►◦►►◦►◦ You're It!: The Playground and Beyond

In the same way that hammers and saws are useful for building houses, stories are useful as tools for thinking about the world. Oftentimes, justice gets its first test on the playground or in the classroom. Ideas of fairness can start with something as simple as dividing a chocolate bar in half, deciding on whether to cheat on a test, or whether a person can take back a gift after it is given. This section offers stories that people have used to think through these practical questions of justice. We hope that you will find them useful too.

The Wise King

(United States)

Speaking of justice, what is the best way to split a chocolate bar between two friends? The playground bully will often divide it into two unequal pieces and give you the smaller piece. But there are some old tricks you can use to ensure fairness. The king in this story knows that well.

O nce there was a wise king who had grown old and tired. He knew the time had come to divide his land between his two sons. The older prince was a fierce warrior but a selfish soul. The younger was a prince of a man, gentle, kind, and loving. His first son was intent on ruling the entire kingdom, but the king had decided to divide his property equally between them. He devised a clever plan. He told the older son to go through the land and determine how it could be divided fairly between him and his brother.

When the king's younger son learned of the plan,

he approached his father's throne. "Father," he said, "why have you asked my brother to decide how the land should be divided? He is not known for his just predisposition."

The wise king smiled at his son. "I have my reasons," he said.

The older son went through the land and found a convenient place to draw a line that would give him the best and biggest part of the kingdom. The piece he intended for himself ran along the river, and included all of the fertile land in the kingdom. To his brother he assigned the eastern portion, which had the swamp and mountain ranges, where no crops could ever grow.

The wise king asked the older son, "Have you divided the land fairly?"

"Yes, my father, I have divided it well."

———————————————

Can you guess the king's plan?

"Ah," said the king, "since you have divided it fairly, I will let your brother choose the piece he wants."

• • • •

Have you ever said to a friend, "Okay, you divide the chocolate bar in half and then I'll choose the piece I want"? Suddenly, rather than taking six squares for himself and giving you two, your friend will painstakingly break off two portions that are exactly equal. The same wisdom that helped a wise king divide his kingdom can help you divide a candy bar!

Josephus in the Cave

(Ancient Israel)

If you and your friends are playing hide-and-seek, how do you decide who will be "it"? Sometimes, one of the players volunteers and the choice is easy. But if no one wants the job, you might decide by playing a counting-out game, like "one potato, two potato, three potato, four." Counting-out games can be found all over the world. Here is one from Uganda in which children name objects such as coffee cans and animals such as lizards in a nonsense rhyme to decide who is "it":

> Kannemu, kannabiri,
> Kafumba, mmwanyi,
> Katta, kkonbkome,
> Malanajja, kannakkwale,
> Ofumba otya kulujjo.

In this game, children sit in a circle with their legs stretched out in front of them. As they recite the rhyme, one person counts around the circle, each word corresponding to a leg. On the word kulujjo, *the person whose outstretched leg is pointed to must tuck it under him- or herself. The rhyme is then repeated. The winner is the last child who still has a leg stretched out.*

In Puerto Rico, fingers are counted:

> Pico pico mandorico,
> Quién te dió el baño de pico
> A la vuelta, a la redonda,
> Esta mano que se esconda!

The language and words are different, but all of these games provide a system for choosing that feels fair and impartial. Yet, there are also many ways to cheat or devise strategies for beating the system—to make sure that you are not "it" if you don't want to be, or to be sure that you get to choose a particular member for your team.

A folklorist named Elliot Oring wrote an essay about a well-known episode in biblical history. Along with a number of other writers through history, he suggests that the hero of the story cheated at a kind of counting-out game to save his life. This is our retelling of that famous episode.

I n ancient times, soon after the birth of Jesus, a controversial Jewish leader named Flavius Josephus visited Rome. Rome ruled Israel at the time, and Josephus was awed by its military might. When the Jews launched a rebellion against Rome in the year 66, he was asked to serve as general of the army of Galilee (Israel). Although he believed their cause to be hopeless, he took command. In the year 67, Josephus directed the defense of the town of Jotapata against the marauding Romans.

Sure enough, the Romans overran Galilee, and broke through the walls of Jotapata. Jewish fighters suffered massive casualties. When the city fell, Josephus fled with six men to a cave. Besieged by Roman troops, they were unwilling to surrender.

One of Josephus's soldiers, lying wounded on the ground, declared, "I won't be taken alive." Two other soldiers agreed, and soon all the men joined in the chorus.

Josephus was not inclined to die for the cause, but he recognized that he would have to go along with his brave men, or else seem a coward.

Josephus took command of the situation. "Men,"

he said, "we have no poison to end our lives and spite our enemies. It is much too hard to kill oneself. We will have to kill one another. The seven of us will stand in a line. The first in line will put his sword through the second man. The third man in line will kill the person who is fourth, and so on. When we get to the end of the line, we will start back in the other direction. The last man left will kill himself."

———————————————————————————————

Josephus had a plan up his sleeve. Where do you think he stood in the line to make sure that he survived?

As the men formed the killing line, Josephus shuffled himself into the third position. Soldier number 1 killed soldier number 2, soldier 3 (Josephus) killed soldier 4, then 5 killed 6.

Moving back the other way, 7 killed 5, and 3 (Josephus) killed 1.

Only 7 and 3 (Josephus) were left. According to the rules, it was number 3's (Josephus's) turn to kill 7.

Here is a diagram of how things stood:

round one: ①② ③④ ⑤⑥ ⑦

round two: ①③ ⑤⑦

round three: ③ ⑦

Did Josephus kill the other surviving soldier and then himself? No way. According to Josephus's writings, when he was left alone with one other man, the two agreed not to kill each other, and escaped by cover of night. Josephus lived to write the history of the rebellion many years later.

Josephus became a Roman sympathizer and a historian. His writings about the Jewish uprising are the only extended account of the events by a writer of that time. He tells about the episode in the cave, and in one manuscript confesses that he "counted the numbers with cunning, and thereby misled them all." Although he lived almost two thousand years ago, many still debate whether he was a loyal Jew or a traitor.

In the actual historical account, Josephus entered the cave with forty other soldiers. Mathematicians have studied the system he might have devised in a split second to assure his survival with forty-one men in the cave. If it is this difficult to figure out where to stand with seven men, imagine the difficulties when there are forty-one!

• • • •

Do you think it's fair to be so methodical? When kids are choosing up sides, they often want to allow pure luck to determine who will be the captain, who will choose first, or who will be "it." Is it fair to devise a system in which you will always win?

The Water Pot and the Necklace

(N i g e r i a)

This wonderful African folktale raises issues with which everyone is familiar from their earliest days on the playground. We first learned this story from Raouf Mama, a storyteller from Benin. "The Water Pot and the Necklace" is a story about jealousy. It raises questions about whether "one bad deed deserves another" and about whether it is "fair" to take back a gift you have given. You may need a bit of King Solomon's wisdom to solve it.

O nce in a village in Nigeria there lived two young girls. Their names were Ashabi and Alaté, and they were the best of friends. They grew up together and married two men from the same village. One day, Ashabi found a kola nut and planted it. The kola tree began to bear fruit, but animals from the village came to eat the leaves and nibble at its roots. Ashabi loved the tree very much, and she wanted to keep it safe.

Then Alaté found a water pot. The bottom had broken off, but it had no other cracks or scratches. It was perfectly round and open on both ends. Alaté could put her arm right through it. That afternoon, she gave the water pot to Ashabi. "Here," she said, "you can put this over your tree. Now it will be protected from the animals and insects." Ashabi hugged her friend and thanked her. The tree grew now, for Ashabi loved it and cared for it well. By selling the kola nuts, she even began to acquire some wealth and possessions of her own.

As time passed, Alaté began to look at her friend with envy. "Ashabi will soon be the wealthiest woman in the village!" she thought to herself. So she came before Ashabi and said, "I want the top of my water pot back. Please give it to me." Ashabi replied, "I would be happy to give it back to you, but I can't do that without cutting down the tree."

"Still," said Alaté, "that is my water pot and I want it back—just as it was—with no cracks or scratches on it." They brought the matter before the chief. He listened and then he ruled: "The pot first belonged to Alaté, who gave it to you. It must be returned."

So Ashabi had to cut down the tree. She grieved for it bitterly.

A year later, Alaté gave birth to her first child, a daughter. On her naming day, Ashabi went to her friend's house and gave the baby a gift, a necklace made of a single piece of brass that was molded to fit her neck perfectly. Alaté thanked her and put the necklace on the child. The girl grew up, and when she was ten years old, Ashabi came before Alaté and said, "I want my necklace back. Please give it to me." Alaté replied, "But my daughter wears the necklace every day."

Ashabi said, "Still, it is mine, and I want it back, just as I gave it to you—whole, with no marks on it." Alaté moaned, "But the child has grown. I can't give it back to you without cutting off my daughter's head!" So they took the matter before the chief.

The chief was a wise man, familiar with the wisdom of the elders and his ancestors. He remembered what happened years before with Ashabi's kola nut tree, and how Alaté had demanded her pot back, causing the death of the tree. Now the two women had come before him again, with the question of Ashabi's necklace.

What should the chief do? How would you decide this matter?

The chief devised a plan. He called the man who conducted the executions into his tent, and explained the situation and what he wanted him to do. Then he called the two women together.

"Yes," he said, "Ashabi is just in her claim. If Alaté could force Ashabi to cut down the kola tree to reclaim her water pot, then Ashabi can force Alaté to put her daughter to death so that she may reclaim her necklace. Cut off her head!" the chief declared solemnly. The executioner lifted up his ax and held it to the skies, his arms frozen like a statue. Suddenly, tears sprang to Ashabi's eyes. She leaped forward and put her arm around the child. "Please don't kill her," she cried. "I was angry about my kola nut tree, but it is not the child's fault. No, I do not want to return bad for bad, for only more bad will come of it. Please let her go." The chief nodded, and the executioner lowered his ax to the ground.

So the child was saved.

In time, the two women who had always been friends could be seen walking through the village with Alaté's daughter between them, selling nuts from a kola tree they had planted together.

· · · ·

This story reminds us of the famous tale about King Solomon. Two women each claimed to be the mother of a baby boy. Solomon commanded that the baby be cut in half, assuming that the real mother would never let that happen.

By his actions, the chief was able to teach Ashabi and Alaté that a gift is a gift. Have you ever had the experience of giving away a possession and then regretting it? When we see how much a friend enjoys our gift, we can't help thinking, "If it's really that great, maybe I should have kept it for myself." Offering a gift is one of life's greatest pleasures. We often wrap gifts to signify that they are special, and that the one who receives the gift does not have to give anything back. A gift giver demands nothing in return. If a gift can be taken back, it's not a gift at all. It's a loan.

The Test

(United States)

Philip Raible, a trial lawyer in New York City, passed this story on to our editor, Marc Aronson, who told it to us. Philip found this story on the Internet, which enables stories to travel all around the globe in a moment's time. It was related as a true story, but we leave it up to you to decide if it really happened.

Once there were two students, Jay Radburn and Mike Kinally, who attended Duke University. Both were history majors specializing in the twentieth century. In their American History course, the grade for the class hinged on the final exam, which covered the two world wars and was scheduled for Monday morning at nine o'clock. Although both of them loved to party, they were also good students who had the ability to pull what is called an "all-nighter." That is, you stay up until morning and cram for a test, covering months of work in a single night.

Now, the night before the final exam was Jay's birthday, and his friends threw a big party for him that went late into the night. The party wound down at about two in the morning. Jay and Mike were exhausted. The two students decided to get just one hour of sleep and then wake up and study for the rest of the night, right up until the exam, at 9:00 A.M. Mike asked Jay to set his alarm clock, but as soon as Jay hit the bed he was out like a light.

When Jay woke up, it was 9:15 in the morning. He woke Mike and they both looked at each other, as if to say, "Uh-oh, what do we do now?" They were already late for the test, so they fried some eggs and sat down to eat. Over breakfast they hatched a plan.

They ran to the exam hall, getting there just as the test was finishing. "Dr. Mahoney," Mike said, completely out of breath, "we've had an absolutely terrible night. We were away for the weekend at Myrtle Beach and drove back last night. In the middle of the night we had a flat tire. We didn't have a spare in the car, so we ended up walking for an hour to find a phone, and it took three hours before the mechanic reached us. The long and the short of it is, we just made it here."

To their delight and surprise, Dr. Mahoney was remarkably understanding. "Just come back tomorrow and I'll give you a makeup exam."

"It worked!" Mike exclaimed as they walked back to their dorm. Now they were just where they wanted to be—with a whole night to learn everything about World War I and World War II. They stayed up all night, cramming, and arrived at the exam hall exhausted but ready at 9:00 A.M.

"Since I can't be here to monitor you, I'm going to put you each in a separate room," Dr. Mahoney told them. He gave them their exam sheets and their "blue books" for their answers. When Jay and Mike opened their exam sheets, they saw there was only one question on the test.

_____

What was the question?

The question consisted of only two words: "Which tire?"

Epilogue

All of these stories, as they have been told and passed on, give one solution, but you and your friends might think of others. Whatever you decide, you will be participating in a process—in a way of thinking—that has enabled people to try to live together in harmony and trust for countless generations. Martin Luther King, Jr., once said, "True peace is not merely the absence of tension. It is the presence of justice."

According to ancient Egyptian legend, a boat carried recently departed souls to the goddess Maat and the scales of justice in the Land of the Dead. Only if their souls balanced perfectly against the goddess Maat's fabled ostrich feather of justice were they allowed to proceed. Here in the land of the living, it's up to each of us to carry our own scales of justice in a corner of our minds. Throughout our lives, when we weigh the evidence, we are not only judging other people but ourselves and our own sense of fairness. For, as it is told in a story from West Africa, the rooster crows every morning to remind us all that there is such a thing as justice in the world.

Source Notes

Introduction   Descriptions of Egyptian myths and symbols were based on material in *The Gods of the Egyptians: A Study in Egyptian Mythology* and *The Egyptian Book of the Dead (The Papyrus of Ani): Egyptian Text, Transliteration and Translation*, both by E. A. Wallis Budge, who collected and studied these ancient documents under the auspices of the British Museum around the beginning of the twentieth century. The quote by Clarence Darrow appears in his book *Attorney for the Damned*, published in 1924.

Poetic Justice:
A Taste of Their Own Medicine

The Cow of No Color   Thanks to Emanuel Ackumey, staff member of the Ghana Mission in New York City, for providing background information and linguistic references. Impossible requests that are responded to in kind may be found in other tales as well, such as "The Fire on the Mountain," in *The Fire on the Mountain and Other Ethiopian Stories*, by Harold Courlander; "The Case of the Boiled Egg," in *While Standing on One Foot: Puzzle Stories and Wisdom Tales from the Jewish Tradition*, by Nina Jaffe and Steve Zeitlin; and "The Hunter," in *African Myths and Legends*, edited by Susan Feldman. A discussion of the use of proverbs among the Anang of Nigeria appears in John C. Messenger's essay "The Role of Proverbs in a Nigerian Judicial System," in *The Study of Folklore*, edited by Alan Dundes.

The Sound of Work   The motif of "sound for smell" is found in many folktales and literary texts going as far back as the sixteenth century, including an episode featuring "Pierre le Fou" (Pierre the Fool) in the work *Pantagruel*, by the French Renaissance writer Rabelais. *In the Month of Kislev: A Story for Hannukah*, by Nina Jaffe, is based on an Ashkenazic (Eastern European Jewish) version of this tale set in the shtetl life of Poland. For more folktales and background on Joha (alternate spelling: Djuha) see *Arab Folktales*, translated and edited by Inea Bushnaq. A version of "The Sound of Work" is also included in *Because God Loves Stories: An Anthology of Jewish Storytelling*, edited by Steve Zeitlin.

Ximen Bao and the River Spirit According to historians, the events in this story happened during the era of the warrior states, 475–221 B.C.E., when China was broken up into different countries, each warring against the other. Ximen Bao lived during that time, and stories about him continue to be told in Taiwan and the People's Republic of China.

The Cloak A Jewish version of this story, "The Divided Cloak," can be found in *A Portion in Paradise and Other Jewish Folktales*, compiled by H. M. Nahmad. A shorter version, "Half a Blanket," which was collected in 1963, appears in Henry Glassie's collection *Irish Folktales*. Joseph Bruchac discusses and tells a Native American (Mohawk) version, "The Other Half of the Blanket," in his book *Tell Me a Tale*. Mayer Kirschenblatt also tells a version in an interview conducted in 1984 for the documentary film *The Grand Generation*.

Bringing Wrongdoers to Justice:
Matters of Guilt and Innocence

The Thief and the Pig This story can be found in *Stories about Quick-Wittedness and Schemes in Chinese Folktales*, edited by Tan Qi. We are indebted to Li Chi Ho, a graduate student at Bank Street College of Education, for sharing her unpublished version and for providing important background information and references on Chinese history and culture in the retelling of this tale.

The Testimony of the Fly Thanks to the Center for Southeast Asian Studies at the University of Wisconsin for background materials on Vietnamese history and culture, and to the Center for Folk Arts in Education in New York City for the source *From Rice Paddies and Temple Yards: Traditional Music of Vietnam*, by Phong Thuyet Nguyen and Patricia Shehan Campbell. The story also appears in Jane Yolen's collection *Favorite Folktales from Around the World*.

Susannah and the Elders This story from the Apocrypha appears in *Law: A Treasury of Art and*

Literature, edited by Sara Robbins. The story of Susannah appears as a theme in the work of artists and composers from the Renaissance to contemporary times; for example, Tintoretto's famous painting *Susannah and the Elders* (circa 1555), and Paul Hindemith's chorale *Sancta Susanna* (1921).

The Jury   In the summer of 1986, folklorist Sam Schrager recorded this story during a program on "American Trial Lawyers" that he curated at the Smithsonian Institution's Festival of American Folklife. The program highlighted trial lawyers as storytellers and demonstrated the craft of storytelling as it is used in the courtroom. Sam has written a book about the subject, *Performing Justice: The Appearance of Truth in Trial Lawyers' Art*, which is forthcoming from Temple University Press.

Forgiveness and Mercy:
Throwing the First Stone

The Magic Seed   A Jewish version, "The Pomegranate Seed," appears in *A Portion in Paradise and Other Jewish Folktales*, compiled by H. M. Nahmad. A version from China, "The Pear Tree," is included in the excellent collection *Fair Is Fair: World Folktales of Justice*, edited by Sharon Creeden. Creeden's book, which came out while this work was in progress, also finds the association to the New Testament story in which Jesus, being tested on his knowledge of the law, successfully defends a woman who has been condemned to death. In her book, Creeden, a lawyer turned storyteller, points out interesting connections between folktales and particular cases in the legal system.

The Bird Lovers Yamy Vang, who told us this story, left Laos when she was still a small child. She later received a grant to study Hmong embroidery traditions with her aunt, a distinguished story-cloth artist. For more information on this tradition, see *Stories in Thread: Hmong Pictorial Embroidery*, by Marsha MacDowell.

An Ounce of Mud A version of this story, "What Tipped the Scales," is included in *A Treasury of Jewish Folklore*, edited by Nathan Ausubel. The theme of the soul's judgment in a heavenly court is found in many Jewish folktales and religious texts. A Hasidic story, "Levi Yitzchak Burns the Evidence," which includes the image of the divine scales, can be found in *Because God Loves Stories: An Anthology of Jewish Storytelling*, edited by Steve Zeitlin.

Settling Disputes:
Between a Rock and a Hard Place

The Dance of Elegba This story is current in the Yoruba tradition of Ifá divination in both Nigeria and Cuba, as well as in the Yoruba-Christian tradition. A reference to this story appears in *Flash of the Spirit: African and Afro-American Art and Philosophy*, by Robert Farris Thompson. One complete version can be found in *Esu-Elegba: Ifá and the Divine Messenger*, by Awo Fá'lokun Fatunmbi. A retelling for young readers, "The Test of Friendship," appears in *The Dancing Palm Tree and Other Tales from Nigeria*, by Barbara K. Walker. Other stories about Elegba can be found in Harold Courlander's book *Tales of Yoruba Gods and Heroes*. Many thanks to Judith Gleason and to Paulo Bispo of the Caribbean Cultural Center in New York City for providing important scholarly references. John Taiwo Odusote, a staff member of the Nigerian

Consulate in New York, kindly told me his version of the story, and supplied the names of the two farmers, Olufemi (which means "God loves me") and Olushegun ("God wins").

The Three Wives of Nenpetro This dilemma tale is included in Susan Feldman's collection *African Myths and Legends* as "How the Wives Restored Their Husband to Life." The theme of characters with different powers bringing a lost person back to life can be found in such tales as "The Cowtail Switch" and "How Anansi Was Saved from the River," both in Harold Courlander's *A Treasury of African Folklore*. A Dagomba version, "Three Wives," can be found in *African Folktales*, by Roger D. Abrahams.

The Flask This story was told to Steve by Rabbi Edward Schecter. It also appears in a book called *Midrashic Rabbinic Lore*, by Harry Gersh, with "Study Questions" by Dr. Robert L. Platzner. Nina heard and discussed this story as a child in Hebrew school at Park Avenue Synagogue in New York City. It is still being told and used today in Jewish education programs and classrooms.

Deciding Ownership: Who Owns the Sky?

Kim Son Dal and the Water-Carriers *The Story of Kim Son Dal*, by Mark C. K. Setton, is a picture-book version of the tale. Many thanks to the Korean Cultural Services Library in New York City for providing assistance in research and background information; and to Professor Young Kyun Oh, lecturer of Korean, Department of East Asian Literature at the University of Wisconsin, for providing historical details and discussing Kim Son Dal's role and function in Korean folklore.

The Land This story from the Talmud appears in *Judaism and Vegetarianism*, by Richard Schwartz. Schwartz also cites a retelling by Rabbi Shlomo Riskin in the film *Biblical Ecology: A Jewish View*, by Mitchell Chalek and Jonathan Rosen. Nina remembers seeing an Islamic version of the story in which Nasreddin, a wise man in the folklore of the Middle East and Turkey, solves the dispute. Unfortunately, she has not been able to locate the reference.

Cosmic Justice: The Big Questions

Sharing the Soup Thanks to Mari Haas, director of Project PLUMA at Teachers College, Columbia University, for background research and references, and to Rachel Kramer, Spanish teacher at the Town School, in New York City, for background on the Day of the Dead festival. A written version of this story, "The Hungry Peasant, God and Death," collected in the Mexican state of Zacatecas, appears in *A Treasury of Mexican Folkways*, edited by Frances Toor.

A Higher Truth Our chief source for this retelling appears as "The Truth" in Inea Bushnaq's definitive volume, *Arab Folktales*. She heard some of these tales as a child in Palestine, and for her book she drew on folk stories that she collected along with the work of previous Arabic and western folklorists. The story in our book was first collected by Hans Schmidt, working with the German Protestant Archaeological Institute in 1910 and 1911.

The Walnut and the Pumpkin A. K. Ramanujan's source for this story was Knowles, *Folktales of*

Kashmir. Indian folklore is rich with many wisdom tales such as the ancient collection *The Panchatantra*, which is made up of stories that were told to educate young Brahmin princes in how to rule wisely.

You're It!: The Playground and Beyond

The Wise King   This story is drawn from Steve's experiences on the playground as a child and a fragment of a tale he remembered from his work on Jewish folklore.

Josephus in the Cave   Many of the writings of Josephus have been preserved and translated from the original Greek. A recommended text of his most well-known work is *Josephus: The Jewish Wars*, edited by Gaalyahu Kornfeld. Elliot Oring's essay was delivered at the 1996 meeting of the American Folklore Society and appears in *Western Folklore*, vol. 56, 1997. The counting game from Uganda is included in Susan M. Durojaiye's article "Children's Traditional Games and Rhymes in Three Cultures," in *Educational Research* (vol. 19, no. 3). Emma Kiwuwa of the Consulate of Uganda in New York City kindly provided a translation. The Puerto

Rican counting-out rhyme was collected at the Grand Street Settlement House in New York City in 1988.

The Water Pot and the Necklace   Thanks to George Soyeju of the Nigerian Consulate in New York City for consulting on Yoruba language and names. "Don't Pay Bad for Bad," a version by the late Nigerian novelist Amos Tutuola, appears in *Jump Up and Say!: A Collection of Black Story-telling*, edited by Linda and Clay Goss.

The Test   We are pleased to include a story from the newest form of "oral tradition." Actually, it's the written tradition of the Internet. A story can get around so quickly on the Internet that by the time you see a story there and tell your friends, they may have already heard it.

Epilogue   The full story referred to here, in which the rooster crows for justice, appears in *Tales of Mogho: African Stories from Upper Volta*, by Frederic Guirma, under the title "The War of the Animals Against the Birds." The quote attributed to Martin Luther King, Jr., can be found in his book

Stride Toward Freedom: The Montgomery Story. A slightly different version of this quote ("Peace is not only the absence of war, but rather the presence of active justice," which appears in the 1996 annual bulletin of Educators for Social Responsibility, in New York City) has also been attributed to South African leader Alan Bozak.

Bibliography

◇◇◇◇◇◇

Abrahams, Roger D. *African Folktales: Traditional Stories of the Black World.* New York: Random House, 1983.

Ausubel, Nathan, ed. *A Treasury of Jewish Folklore.* New York: Crown Publishers, 1948, 1975.

Bruchac, Joseph. *Tell Me a Tale.* New York: Harcourt and Brace, 1997.

Budge, E. A. Wallis. *The Gods of the Egyptians: A Study in Egyptian Mythology.* New York: Dover Publications, 1904, 1969.

————. *The Egyptian Book of the Dead (The Papyrus of Ani): Egyptian Text, Transliteration and Translation.* New York: Dover Publications, 1895, 1967.

Bushnaq, Inea, ed. *Arab Folktales*. New York: Pantheon Books, 1987.

Campos, Anthony John. *Mexican Folk Tales*. Tucson, Ariz.: University of Arizona Press, 1977, 1996.

Courlander, Harold. *A Treasury of African Folklore*. New York: Crown Publishers, 1975; Marlowe and Co., 1995.

————. *Tales of Yoruba Gods and Heroes*. New York: Crown Publishers, 1973; Fawcett, 1974.

————. *On Recognizing the Human Species*. New York: Anti-Defamation League/One Nation Library, 1960.

Creeden, Sharon, ed. *Fair Is Fair: World Folktales of Justice*. Little Rock, Ark.: August House, 1994.

Dundes, Alan, and Alison Dundes Renteln, eds. *Folk Law*, vols. I and II. Madison, Wis.: University of Wisconsin Press, 1994.

Durojaiye, Susan M. "Children's Traditional Games and Rhymes in Three Cultures," *Educational Research*, vol. 19, no. 3.

Fatunmbi, Awo Fá'lokun. *Esu-Elegba: Ifá and the Divine Messenger*. Plainview, N.J.: Original Publications (undated).

Feldman, Susan, ed. *African Myths and Legends*. New York: Dell, 1963.

Gersh, Harry. *Midrashic Rabbinic Lore*. (With "Study Questions" by Dr. Robert L. Platzner.) New York: Behrman House, 1985.

Glassie, Henry. *Irish Folktales*. New York: Random House, 1985.

Golding, M. P., ed. *The Nature of Law: Readings in Legal Philosophy*. New York: Random House, 1966.

Goss, Linda and Clay, eds. *Jump Up and Say!: A Collection of Black Storytelling*. New York: Simon and Schuster, 1995.

Guirma, Frederic. *Tales of Mogho: African Stories from Upper Volta*. New York: Macmillan Company, 1971.

Jaffe, Nina. *The Mysterious Visitor: Stories of the Prophet Elijah*. New York: Scholastic, 1997.

———. *In the Month of Kislev: A Story for Hanukkah*. New York: Viking Children's Books, 1992.

Jaffe, Nina, and Steve Zeitlin. *While Standing on One Foot: Puzzle Stories and Wisdom Tales from the Jewish Tradition*. New York: Henry Holt and Co., 1993.

Kairys, David, ed. *The Politics of Law: A Progressive Critique*. New York: Pantheon Books, 1982.

Kalman, Bobbie. *Mexico: Su Tierra; Mexico: Su Gente*. New York: Crabtree Publishing Co., 1994.

Macdonald, Margaret. *The Storyteller's Source Book*. Detroit, Mich.: Neil-Schuman Publishers, 1982.

May, Herbert G., and Bruce M. Metzger. *The Oxford Annotated Bible*. New York: Oxford University Press, 1962.

Messenger, John C. "The Role of Proverbs in a Nigerian Judicial System," in Alan Dundes, ed., *The Study of Folklore*. Englewood Cliffs, N.J.: Prentice-Hall, 1965.

Nahmad, H. M., ed. *A Portion in Paradise and Other Jewish Folktales*. New York: Schocken Books, 1974.

Nguyen, Phong Thuyet, and Patricia Shehan Campbell. *From Rice Paddies and Temple Yards: Traditional Music of Vietnam*. Danbury, Conn.: World Music Press, 1990, 1991.

Ramanujan, A. K. *Folktales from India*. New York: Pantheon Books, 1991.

Robbins, Sara. *Law: A Treasury of Art and Literature*. New York: Hugh Lauter Levin Associates, 1990.

Roth, Cecil, ed. *Encyclopedia Judaica*, vols. 3, 5, and 15. Jerusalem (Israel): Keter Publishing House, 1972.

Schwartz, Richard. *Judaism and Vegetarianism*. Smithtown, N.Y.: Exposition Press, 1982.

Schwarzbaum, Haim. *Jewish Folklore Between East and West: Collected Papers*. Edited and with an introduction by Eli Yasif. Beer-Sheeva (Israel): Ben Gurion University of the Negev Press, 1989.

Setton, Mark C. K. *The Story of Kim Son Dal*. Seoul (Korea): Si-sa-yong-o-sa, Inc., 1985.

Tan Qi, ed. *Stories about Quick-Wittedness and Schemes in Chinese Folktales* (in Chinese), vols. 19 and 20. Taipei (Taiwan): Hinyi (no date).

Tapp, June Loun, and Felice J. Levine, ed. *Law, Justice and the Individual in Society: Psychological and Legal Issues*. New York: Holt, Rinehart and Winston, 1977.

Thompson, Robert Farris. *Flash of the Spirit: African and Afro-American Art and Philosophy*. New York: Random House, 1983.

Toor, Frances, ed. *A Treasury of Mexican Folkways*. New York: Crown Publishers, 1964.

Urquhart, Sir Thomas, and Pierre Le Motteux, trans. *Rabelais: Gargantua and Pantagruel*. Vol. II. New York: AMS Press, Inc., 1967.

Vo-Dinh, Mai. *The Toad Is the Emperor's Uncle: Animal Tales from Vietnam*. New York: Doubleday and Co., 1970.

Walker, Barbara K. *The Dancing Palm Tree and Other Tales from Nigeria*. Lubbock, Tex.: Texas Tech University Press, 1990.

Yolen, Jane, ed. *Favorite Folktales from Around the World.* New York: Pantheon Books, 1986.

Zeitlin, Steve, ed. *Because God Loves Stories: An Anthology of Jewish Storytelling.* New York: Simon and Schuster, 1997.

Resources and Organizations

Here are organizations that work for peace, justice, and human rights through educational outreach, publications, and advocacy.

Educators for Social Responsibility
23 Garden Street
Cambridge, MA 02138
(617) 492-1764

Facing History and Ourselves
16 Hurd Road
Brookline, MA 02146
(617) 232-1595

Teaching Tolerance: A Publication of the Southern
    Poverty Law Center
400 Washington Avenue
Montgomery, AL 36104

Further resources in folklore and storytelling:

The Center for Folk Arts in Education
A Bank Street/City Lore Collaboration
72 East First Street
New York, NY 10003

The National Storytelling Association
P.O. Box 309
Jonesboro, TN 37659